A Pennine Childhood

Brenda Wallis Smith

D1114252

ISBN: 1484195671
ISBN 13: 9781484195673

Library of Congress Control Number: 2013908292
CreateSpace Independent Publishing Platform
North Charleston, South Carolina

For my daughters Virginia and Susan,
and grandchildren Katie, John, Meg, and Jessica
With Love

Table of Contents

PART 1

1928-1937

The Derwent Valley

The Derwent Valley
Derbyshire, England

Bakewell

Matlock

Matlock Bath

Lea

Lea Bridge

Cromford

Holloway

A6

Crich

Wirksworth

Whatstandwell

Alderwasley

Fritchley

River

Bullbridge

Derwent

Ambergate

Belper

1 mi.

Derby

CHAPTER 1

The Valley

5, Matlock Road, fifty years on

I WAS BORN ON the twenty-third of May, 1928, in the front bedroom of 5, Matlock Road, Ambergate, where Derbyshire's Derwent River runs through the southern foothills of the Pennine Chain to converge with the River Amber. As a small child, looking west from my bedroom, I could see the busy A6 road to Matlock, and beyond it, behind a row of houses, the meadows that stretched down to the riverbank. Rising up a hill on the far side, Chase Wood stretched all the way along the river to Whatstandwell. There grew conifers, oak, ash, sycamore, and beech along with, in season, drifts of bluebells and armies of foxgloves. When I raised my head, I could see above the trees more fields where Ayrshire and Holstein cattle nibbled and tore at the grass.

Augmented, no doubt, by my newborn howls, Ambergate was not a quiet place. Just beyond our front garden, buses, cars, motorbikes, and lorries roared past, spewing exhaust fumes which, coupled with smoke from our coal fires, filled the valley from November to March with fog. On summer weekends, the swish of bikes and the cries of cyclists came floating into my room as I lay sleepless, the long twilight not yet faded from my window.

Behind the house, trains ran frequently on the bank at the end of our garden, huge iron monsters enveloped in steam and smuts. Those headed for Sheffield made only a faint noise in the distance, but the Manchester trains chuffed and clanked past our garden at least once an hour if they held passengers, and as frequently, but more noisily, when they carried goods. The goods trains often woke us in the night, especially if they were shunting as new wagons were added. These hefty, open wooden boxes had two rounded steel bumpers at each end that crashed metallically into those of the wagons in front and behind whenever the train stopped or backed up. When this happened, the handles on our dresser drawers chimed frantically in unison.

Most of Ambergate is not particularly old. In 1876 the Hurt family, local ironmasters, built the Hurt Arms Hotel just down the road from where Number 5 would stand. Opposite the hotel, a tollhouse keeper collected fees for the Hurt's private roadway to Whatstandwell, now the A6 road to Matlock and beyond.

The canal, between Cromford wharf and Langley Mill, opened in 1794. The Hurts also donated the land where Thewlis Johnson, owner of the local wireworks, gave funds for the construction of the parish church of St Anne's. At the time there were a few older, sandstone cottages in the little community that was then called Toadmoor, but the later, brick houses were built after the 1840s when the railway arrived, ours as late as the 1920s. By 1931 the population reached nine hundred and one, and the railway junction had been named Amber Gate.

Ours was one in a row of ten semidetached brick and pebble-dash houses put up by a local builder to house, among others, the clerks who worked on the railway or in the county offices in Derby. Our house, like all the rest, had two main rooms downstairs, a sitting and a dining room, with the addition of a scullery and a pantry under the stairs 'where the gas meter ticked', as Dylan Thomas has it. Upstairs was a bathroom, the front and back bedrooms, and my box room that overlooked the A6 road. The room was tiny, about six by eight feet, with a single bed, a small dressing table, and on the wall a picture my Grandmother Wallis had given me of a farmyard with hens and a cockerel. It was the room I thought of when at school I learned the poem 'I remember, I remember/The house where I was born/The little window where the sun/Came creeping in at morn.' This was despite the fact that my window faced due west.

Near Ambergate, along the side of the Cromford Canal, rattled and smoked the kilns where limestone from the Crich quarries was burned, and where the trees and grass nearby were rimed in white powder. The sorting of the limestone was a noisy business. Often, when my friend Margaret and I were running in the surrounding fields looking for cowslips, we would hear a loud, metallic rattling as limestone rock was shaken down a long metal tube with holes of different sizes along it. The fragments, now sorted by size, were afterwards burned in a row of eight furnaces where they were reduced to the slaked lime used in farming or the flux essential for removing impurities from lead.

Despite the Depression, the village was a busy place through the 1930s: the home of Johnson's wireworks, Linacre's sawmill, Glossop's brickworks, and Smedley's dye works at Bullbridge. The nearby General Refractories, where bricks and the ganister that was used as a special lining for furnaces were made, employed my father as a commercial traveller.

Many members of my family, the Durwards and the Wallises, still live up and down that portion of the valley that lies between Ambergate and what was then the spa town of Matlock. North of Ambergate, up the Derwent Valley, lie the villages of Whatstandwell, Lea Bridge, Cromford, and the Matlocks, with, on the hills to the west, Alderwasley, and to the east, Fritchley, Crich, Dethick, and Holloway. I spent my early years among these towns and villages, with an occasional foray as far south as Derby; together they formed the border that surrounded my young life.

My father, Jack Wallis, was born at Alderwasley, the eldest of five children. His grandfather had been a gardener and lived with his family at the Bottom Lodge on the Hurt estate; the Hurts had made their fortune from lead during the Industrial Revolution. Dad's father, my grandfather, John Bent Wallis, left school at fourteen.

When only in his twenties and working in the railway offices in Derby, Grandfather, who had a deep love of nature, began his writing career with articles for various local newspapers; later he wrote a daily column, 'The Rambling Naturalist', for the *Sheffield Telegraph*. He was financially supported for a time by one of the Hurts when he was writing the nature column. Also, rather mysteriously, a man named Arkwright, a descendent of Sir Richard, paid him a pension of one pound a year; I have yet to discover why. His diaries, where he kept a record of his sightings of the local flora and fauna, are now kept in the County Archives at Matlock.

My Wallis grandparents and their children lived in several different places close to the Derwent Valley: Alderwasley, Ambergate, Bullbridge, and Crich. They also lived for a while at Buxton, and during Granddad's final years, Whatstandwell.

The Derwent Valley has a great deal of history, and at the age of five or so my grandmother told me the fascinating story of Betty Kenny and her tree. The Hurts needed charcoal for their iron foundries, and this was produced by charcoal burners in the Shining Cliff Woods on the west bank of the Derwent. The family's best-known burners were Luke and Kate Kenny, who were active in the late 1700s. (Kate was later known as Betty, and by some accounts her surname was Kenyon.) They lived in a cone-shaped hut under the branches of a huge yew tree where they brought up their family of eight; in all their lives they never lived in a proper house. They made a cradle for their children in a branch of the tree, and local lore has it that this was the origin of the nursery rhyme 'Rock-a-bye Baby on the Tree Top'. (In the US, I was told that the rhyme alludes to the way the Indians cradled their papooses.)

Both of the Kennys lived to a great age: Luke was ninety-six and Kate eighty-eight when, in 1813, the Hurt of the day employed James Wood, RA, to paint their portraits. The tree—or what is left of it after vandals set fire to it in the '30s—is known locally as Betty Kenny's tree. After Grandfather's death, Grandmother Wallis had his ashes scattered under the tree, as were her own, and later, those of my brothers, Peter and Gilbert.

Opposite Alderwasley, on the east side of the Derwent Valley, are the villages of Whatstandwell and Crich Carr, where the houses follow a narrow winding road up to Crich. From the summit of Crich Stand, the lighthouse-shaped tower, visitors can see all the way to the spires of Lincoln Cathedral. There have been four versions of the Stand over the years: the first was wooden, followed successively by three stone towers. The first stone tower, built by Francis Hurt in 1788, was damaged by lightning, as was the second put up in 1851. In 1923 my husband's uncle, Joe Payne, built the latest tower, which is now a memorial to the Sherwood Foresters. A local story has it that the site was one of the places where, in 1588, bonfires were lit to warn the country that the Spanish Armada was approaching. The limestone, which here protrudes through the surrounding sandstone, has been used for the building of houses since medieval times, and has been the scene of lead mining from Roman times until quite recently; many 'pigs o' lead' have been found nearby.

Further north stands the village of Holloway where the Nightingale family lived with their six children. Their daughter, Florence, born in 1840, was famous for her work among wounded British soldiers during the Crimean War and single-handedly created the profession of nursing. The family spent their summers at Lea Hurst in Holloway and, after she became a nurse, Florence sometimes travelled home by train to Whatstandwell. As was the fashion of the time, Florence was named for the Italian town where she was born, as was her sister Parthenope, who was born in Naples (Parthenope is its Greek name). In the 1870s, my Grandmother Wallis, then Whitehurst, was named for Florence; Grandmother's daughter, Aunt Flo, inherited the name, and finally so did I. Ironically, the Nightingale house was later converted into an old people's home, and Aunt Flo lived there for a time during her later years.

High Peak Junction and the village of Lea Bridge lie in the river valley to the north of Whatstandwell, where John Smedley built his cotton factories in the early eighteenth century to produce the cotton clothing he sent all over the world. There the Cromford and High Peak Railway rises up to the west, enabling Smedley to transport his wares over the hills to Manchester. In her youth, Grandmother Wallis, then Florrie Whitehurst, worked at Smedley's factory; her brother, Ernest, was a foreman. Today, the High Peak Railway is a hiking and birding trail.

Alison Uttley, author of 'The Country Child' and 'Little Grey Rabbit', lived at Hill Top Farm, which overlooked the Derwent just south of Cromford village, and is adjacent to the farm belonging to my Whitehurst family. Grandmother told me that, as a girl, she often encountered her small neighbour as she rode about the countryside on her pony. Professor Denis Judd, Uttley's biographer, reported that Alison 'despised many people', and my grandmother confirmed this, describing her to me as 'stuck up'.

The village of Cromford, further north up the river, was where Richard Arkwright first used run-off from the lead mine soughs (pronounced 'suffs'), to power his looms, the first factories in the world to use waterpower in the spinning of yarn. This helped launch the Industrial Revolution that, for better and for worse, completely changed the way of life for the valley, and eventually for the world.

Beyond Cromford and the small town of Matlock Bath lies the larger Matlock where most of my maternal uncles were employed by the hydros (spas) and other businesses. Uncle George was a doorman at Smedley's Hydro, Uncle Reg a baker for visitors to Rockside Hydro, Uncle Bud a labourer at a nearby farm, later the driver of a milk lorry, and finally a quarryman hacking out sandstone on Matlock Moor. In his lorry-driving days, Bud often took me with him during my school holidays; one of these trips was to collect the day's milk from Barn Close

Farm in Fritchley—the home of the little lad who later became my husband.

Until 1893, Grandfather Durward drove one of the broughams that delivered health-seekers from the railway station, up steep Bank Road, to Smedley's Hydro. When I was a child, Granddad's job was taken over by the trams, and he became a street sweeper for the town. (A local man who had visited San Francisco brought back the idea of using trams to negotiate the steep hill up to the hydro.)

When I was nine, in addition to the stories of Florence Nightingale and the Hurt's charcoal burners told to me by my Wallis grandmother, a teacher enlightened me about the histories of other local families, among them the Babingtons of Dethick. Their son, Anthony, having been appointed page to Mary Queen of Scots when she was imprisoned at Sheffield, became determined to free her, and to this end conspired with other Catholics to assassinate Queen Elizabeth. Babington was apprehended and, in 1586, hanged, drawn, and quartered. Later, in the 1640s, Oliver Cromwell sent his soldiers to attack a Loyalist stronghold at Wingfield Manor, which was also where the Queen of Scots had been imprisoned for a time. On the way, his men bombarded Barn Close Farm, my husband's home in Fritchley. My father-in-law pointed out to me the dents where the Roundhead's cannon balls were said to have hit the walls of his barn.

The teacher, in addition to telling us about Arkwright and his development of the water-powered spinning jenny, spoke of the coming of the railways and canals and the building of roads.

The Derwent Valley is only one of two places in the world where there are four means of transportation in close proximity: a river, a road, a railway, and a canal. The other is in India.

In addition to the Hurt family of Alderwasley, other ironmasters worked at Belper and Milford, while Jedediah Strutt, who had collaborated with Arkwright, developed his own cotton mills at Belper. Further south, Derby had silk mills even before the cotton mills were built, and the town was also home to a famous geologist-cum-clock maker, John Whitehurst, many of whose clocks and other inventions are on display in Derby Museum. Whitehurst was related to my grandmother's family.

A complicated geology of lime and sandstone dominates the area north of Ambergate. (The sandstone is called gritstone or millstone grit locally.) The limestone area, called the White Peak, is mainly on the west side of the Derwent, but also exists as the small hill that pokes its nose above the surrounding gritstone near Crich Stand.

Crich Stand
Copyright The Francis Frith Collection

This is sheep country, and from Roman times until recently, not only the scene of lead mining but also the limestone quarrying that continues to this day. The western limestone area is known for its dales strung along rivers such as the Dove and the Manifold, where grow whitebeam and Guelder rose, lilies of the valley, and wild orchids. Above the dales looms the rocky limestone plateau where jagged white walls surround narrow fields, some of which still show evidence of medieval strip ploughing, their undulating grasses dotted with buttercups, cowslips, bog asphodel, and cotton grass. The yellow-breasted wagtail can be seen there, flocks of rooks and the occasional curlew amid the isolated stands of gnarled oak and ash that seem to cower from the bitter west wind.

On both sides of the River Derwent lies the Dark Peak with its heather-covered moors and rocky gritstone 'edges': the exposed stone that forms craggy walls along the summits of some of the higher hills. Bilberry bushes grow on the moors and the roadsides, and here the little copses have oak, ash, sycamore, and beech, along with the occasional horse chestnut. On the lower elevations, towards the river, the farms produce cattle and wheat, and there is much sandstone quarrying. Queen Anne's lace flourishes under the sandstone walls, along with foxglove and goldenrod. Hawks and skylarks can be seen above the moorland, along with robins, starlings, crows, and other common birds.

Before the Industrial Revolution, only the river and a few rough roads used by horsemen and stagecoaches pierced the tranquil valley. Some of those roads were private, and their owners, like the Hurts, demanded tolls. By the end of the eighteenth century, men following Arkwright's lead had opened their own cotton factories, while others developed more iron industries, lead mines, and lime and sandstone quarries, thus adding to the new, local prosperity. All this led to the development of more roads, including the turnpike road to Manchester built in 1815, a continuation of what was the A6 road that ran through our little community.

The Derwent Valley, with its rural beauty, provided woods and fields to run in, bouquets to pick, and tadpoles to capture in my net, along with the excitement of the industrial areas with their rattling lime kilns and the little trains and barges hauling their loads of sandstone and lime from the quarries. My Durward and Wallis families were a part of all this, and it made for me a safe and yet fascinating childhood.

The Derwent River, Matlock

CHAPTER 2
The Wallises

John Bent Wallis

Florence Whitehurst Wallis

GRANDDAD AND GRANNY WALLIS began their married life under a cloud: they eloped. The two were neighbours at the time, the Whitehursts living at a farm called The Kennels in Alderwasley, and Granddad's family nearby at the Hurt's Bottom Lodge near the Derwent River in Whatstandwell. However it happened, Miss Florence Whitehurst and Mr John Bent Wallis walked over the fields one morning to Wirksworth Church and were married.

Granny's family disowned her and would not speak to her for some years. This was the Victorian era with its strict moral code, and marrying without parental consent was frowned upon. Later, the family relented. Family lore is vague about this, but perhaps after the old parents died, the brothers and sisters felt free to acknowledge their wayward sibling.

Grandmother Wallis was a true product of her Victorian upbringing: very upright in her bearing and moral tone, but nevertheless she had a mischievous sense of humour. She was about fifty-five when I first became aware of her, a seemingly old lady with thin, greying hair twisted into a flat bun at the back of her head and clothed in long, almost ankle-length dresses, black or navy with polka dots or tiny flowers. She was also an imperious old lady who, when required to take the outstretched hand of a member of the working class, extended the two fingers that I had recently learned were the required number of digits in a Victorian handclasp between one class and an inferior one. I was a fanciful child, much given to reading history books, and have wondered since if I fabricated that explanation for the handclasp; perhaps two fingers were all that Grandmother's arthritis allowed her to extend. In either case, I saw that working class people seemed to look up to her as some kind of matriarch.

Granddad and Granny Whitehurst and their children:
Florence, Ernest, Rose, Joseph, Henrietta (Etta), and Albert.

Granny had three brothers, only one whom I knew: Uncle Ernest. She also had two sisters: Aunt Rose, who married Gilbert Dewar, a Scotsman, whom she met when working in Scotland as a nanny, and Aunt Henrietta (Etta), who married an older man who shortly thereafter died and left her a widow. She raised her two sons alone, supporting them all by selling Spirella corsets. Once, Aunt Etta came to call at Ambergate with her paraphernalia when Mam was in her late twenties. She and Mam closeted themselves in the front room with the curtains closed, and when the door opened, I had a brief glimpse of Mam standing in her knickers and Aunt Etta kneeling on the floor beside her with a measuring tape. I was not, however, allowed to enter. Corsets were fearsome garments with lots of laces and whalebone supports; they must have prodded the life out of their wearers, but in the twenties and thirties, old ladies of twenty-seven who had given birth to two children were considered more than ready for bolstering by corset.

I met my Great-Granny Whitehurst only once that I remember. She seemed unbelievably old to me and was certainly ill. After a family falling out, she had rented a room at Buckland Hollow in the house that is now the Excavator Pub on the Ripley Road. Great-Granny lay in bed when Granny and I visited her, and I remember that the old lady listened to us through an ear trumpet. Shortly after this, she went to spend her final years with Aunt Etta and her family.

Granddad and his family lived on a farm at Alderwasley when he was young; later, after his father became a gardener on the Hurt estate, the family moved to the Bottom Lodge at Whatstandwell. The Hurts had a Top, Middle, and Bottom Lodge on their estate, each of which housed a keeper or some other servant.

Some of Granddad's paintings are of the house and of various scenes around Alderwasley. After the Wallises had left the Bottom Lodge, it became the scene of one of Granddad's stories. Many years later, as he strolled past the Lodge in his daily pursuit of ideas for his nature column for the *Sheffield Telegraph*, the old woman then living there greeted him. Her young grandson was rampaging about the garden, shouting and brandishing a stick. 'Eh, Mr Wallis,' the old lady said to my grandfather, shaking her head, 'I've riven and striven with that lad, and now 'e's racing round and round the garden shouting pig muck!'

The Bottom Lodge, Whatstandwell

Granddad was a good amateur painter, and the Bottom Lodge was the subject of one of his many paintings. In the Victorian manner, he was self-taught when it came to the natural world; nevertheless his columns were well received. His readers, and people in the different villages where he lived over the years, usually came to revere him. Much later, when I was working as a local librarian, an old lady embarrassed me by loudly referring to Granddad as 'a saint, a positive saint!'

He had a habit of going out very early in the morning and watching, without moving for an hour or more, some natural phenomenon such as a blackbird building its nest or a mole casting up its little hillocks of soil. He was looking for material for his daily column; 'contemplating the beautiful' is what my father called these meditative episodes. The old lady, because she lived near the Cromford Canal where Granddad often took his morning walks, must have witnessed some of these contemplative moments.

In addition to the gravel road that later became the A6 to Buxton and beyond, the Hurts also had jurisdiction over the road that crossed the river by way of the Ha'penny Bridge at Ambergate. There was a little redbrick toll house on the bridge when I was a child where my father and I would stop to pay our ha'penny to the toll house keeper whenever we wanted to drive over the river and up into the hills towards Alderwasley. The house is long gone.

Toll House on the Ha'penny Bridge, Ambergate

Granny and Granddad Wallis had two daughters and three sons. The eldest child was Jack, my father, who was born, as he used to boast, in Queen Victoria's reign. This was only marginally so since Dad was born in 1900, and Victoria died in 1901. Next in age was Arnold, then Ted, followed by the two daughters, Rosie and Flo.

Dad and his brother Arnold Wallis

Uncle Arnold worked for the County Council and later for the Chatsworth estate. Uncle Ted was a traveller for a company that sold agricultural supplies. Rose was the eldest daughter, and from her name I guess that she was born after the family reconciliation, since she was named for my grandmother's sister. The youngest child was Aunt Flo, who took the equivalent of the modern eleven-plus and won a scholarship to Herbert Strutt's Grammar School in Belper.

She was tall, with hazel eyes and straight, dark hair that she wore in a 'bob'. She held a variety of secretarial jobs throughout her life and was known for her efficiency. Oddly, for such a prim woman, when young she belonged to a group that played Hawaiian music in public, her instrument the Hawaiian guitar. It was Flo who assured me that Grandfather's middle name, Bent, referred only to his mother's family name—and a kind of grass. She was very insistent about this.

Granddad Wallis was a handsome man: tall and slender, with a shock of wavy, greying hair and dark brown eyes. He also had the large 'Wallis' nose and a broad, high forehead. He was very quiet and scholarly, interested in and a scholar of everything; he was a typical Victorian. Although he had had no formal education beyond secondary school, he was very widely read. During the war he became bitterly incensed when, as happened occasionally, his nature column was dropped for the day. The editor would explain that because newsprint was in short supply, and because there had been more war news than usual, he had been forced to eliminate Granddad's column. Mam was suspicious of her in-laws ('Think they're somebody!'), and she didn't admire what she considered Granddad's effete calling. 'There's a war on,' she would grumble. 'People want to read about what's happening to their lads!' Granddad, of course, in addition to feeling hurt because his column was dropped, thought that the editor had his values backward. To him, Nature was eternal and of greater import than reports of war.

A View from Alderwasley to Whatstandwell
(JB Wallis)

Grandfather wrote the occasional poem, among them one he composed at the age of thirty-four and addressed to his brother Herbert:

My Brother's Birthday
by
JBW

When I remember all our childish play
Our woodland rambles and our homely joys,
When you and I were careless, happy boys
And Heaven seemed packed into a Summer's day,
I mourn to think how swiftly pass away
Our growing years, and how the radiancies,
Which made the woods and fields a Paradise,
And I am filled with feelings of dismay;
Until remembering that a thousand years
Are to the Unknown but a story told.
At once, a child again, I lose my fears
And trust the Pilot's wisdom manifold
Safe into port to steer our trembling bark
Though suns were dead and all the skies were dark!

Two entries from his diaries read:
15.7.11 Saturday. This date and this day of the week 12 years ago was our wedding day. It was perfect Summertime throughout its golden hours. We went to church in the early morning, walking three miles by

dewy lanes, through mellowing cornfields and flowery pastures. The church (Wirksworth) centuries old, was cool and spacious, with sunshine in bright pools upon the floor. Only the necessary persons were there: next to being married in the glory of God's morning woods, it was ideal. Nay we were wed practically in the open country; far from church windows one saw, not a sordid expanse of chimneys, but sunny slopes and waving trees.

28.4.12 Twelfth anniversary of Jack's birthday. A kindly susceptible lad, quick-tempered as most quick-witted people are, but not an atom of malice about him. Full of interest in the world of Nature and of books, and very discerning. So in their own way, and measure, are his brothers and sisters—even baby Tut (Flo). 'I pray not that thou shouldst take them out of the world, but that thou shouldst keep them from evil.'

Grandfather was nothing if not Victorian.

He was also a kindly man. As a child, I would often visit my grandparents for a week or so during my school holidays and found Granddad to be a lot of fun: teasing, and playing all kinds of board games with me. But one day I raised his ire. Dad's brother, Arnold, suffered from some sort of psychiatric disorder that today would easily be held in check with medicines. In the thirties, however, there were no such refinements, and sufferers were often shunted away into asylums, as was Uncle Arnold for a while. This was not talked of in the family, especially not in front of us children, so I had no idea that my uncle was ill, until the day when I regaled my grandparents with the story of a boy at school who was, I told them, 'completely crackers'.

At this, Granddad lost his temper, telling me how thoughtless, how unkind I was, and that he couldn't believe his granddaughter could be so cruel! He went on in this vein for quite some time, and I was hurt and bewildered; what did Granddad mean when he said I was insulting Uncle Arnold, when I was merely talking about that stupid Byard boy in Standard Four? But Granddad's cheeks were scarlet, his expression furious, and he continued to harangue me for a good five minutes, at the end of which I grabbed my school blazer, stormed out of the house, and walked furiously over the hill to my home in the next village two miles away, where my mother at last enlightened me about my uncle's illness. Grandfather and I made it up the next time I visited, but it was a couple of weeks before I summoned up the courage to return.

Uncle Arnold had always been a favourite with me ever since he had appeared, miraculously it seemed, on the beach at Ballantrae in Scotland and helped me build a sand castle. He had cycled the three hundred miles from Derbyshire, having adopted the new craze for cycling that came after YHA hostels began to spring up all over the country in the early thirties. He had bought his bicycle, he told us, for five pounds.

Unlike his siblings, Uncle Arnold's colouring was quite fair, his eyes blue, although his build was similar to that of my dark-haired father: slim and fairly tall. He never married, and I was never aware of any girlfriends. He spent most of his holidays cycling about the British Isles, either with his sister, my Aunt Flo, or with his men friends. Once, he and Flo turned up at our digs at the village of Looe in Cornwall where we had gone for a holiday. Later in his life, he suffered what was then called a nervous breakdown and spent some time in an asylum after he leaped from his bedroom window, fortunately without injury. In the asylum, he underwent electric shock treatment to the brain, which was believed to help those with his condition. I was not taken to visit him in hospital, but Aunt Flo told me he became very child-like after his treatments. During the war, when still quite young, he died after losing a fight with pneumonia. He was one of my favourite uncles, the first relative I had lost, and I was extremely saddened by his death.

As was usual in our family, death was for adults to deal with. Mam said only 'Bren, Uncle Arnold has died,' adding no words of comfort, or even a hug. However, she had tears in her eyes, and Dad's face was sombre; he and Uncle Arnold had been close ever since they were boys. It was obvious that both my parents were greatly disturbed when a few days later they appeared one afternoon, Mam dressed in her sober black coat and hat, Dad in his grey overcoat with the black band Mam had sewn onto his sleeve, to announce that they were going to Uncle Arnold's funeral. Aunt Gladys would be with us while they were gone; we children were not invited.

Mam had been fond of her brother-in-law, but hostility towards her other in-laws, an outcome of the rigid class distinctions of the 1920s and '30s, had begun during her courtship with my father when Granny Wallis, hearing that her Jack had taken up with someone obscure from Matlock, had gone to the town to make enquiries about her and her family. Mam never forgave her mother-in-law, and thereafter, according to Mam, no member of the Wallis family, apart from Dad and Arnold, could do anything right. Fortunately, Mam's attitude towards the Wallis family had little if any effect on my relationship with them. I loved both my grandparents, as I did all my Durward and Wallis aunts and uncles. I loved them in different ways and degrees and for a variety of reasons, for they were different people, but I tended to block out Mam's opinions of them. Mam was never rude or unwelcoming to her in-laws, but even when quite young, I could sense her distrust of them.

The Beeches, where my Wallis grandparents lived, halfway up Bullbridge Hill on the way to Fritchley, was a wonderful house for a child. To me it seemed very large, much bigger than 5, Matlock Road. It had two big bay windows at the front, a dark, damp cellar, and a pantry where Granny stored the Russet apples she grew in the orchard behind the house. The front rooms of the house had high ceilings and were light and airy, but the orchard, on a bank behind the house, overshadowed the kitchen and pantry windows. Behind the orchard ran the Bottom Hag, which is one of two footpaths that still connect Ambergate and Fritchley. (The other one, the Top Hag, runs parallel a few fields further up the hill.) The garden at the front of the house overlooked Bullbridge Hill down a very steep bank that included a lawn, flowerbeds, and a summerhouse in its far corner.

As many country people did then, Granny kept hens in the orchard, bantams and Rhode Island Reds, and as a small child, it was my delight and fear to go with her to feed them and gather the eggs. If the birds were hungry, they would leave their nests to run outside, but if they were not, I had to brave their beady eyes and ever-ready beaks, ease my hand under their warm bottoms and sneak out their eggs. I felt that they resented me and were waiting for Granny's back to be turned before they attacked. They never did, although my grandmother often had to whoosh away the fierce cockerel with her pinafore.

When I was a child, Uncle Arnold and Aunts Flo and Rosie were still living at home; only Dad and Uncle Ted were married at the time. People invariably stayed with their families until they married and lived in houses of their own; when single 'getting away from home' to one's own flat was almost unheard of in a small village such as ours. As for 'living in sin', it was probably very rare; in London it was different, but in the hinterland mores were still tinged with Victorianism, especially in the Wallis family.

Visiting The Beeches was a weekly Sunday morning affair. 'Jack's getting his bottle filled', Aunt Gladys would mock, insinuating a return to Mammy. Dad's car was an old Jowett that had running boards, celluloid windows, and very little power. To my terror, it would usually not make it up Bullbridge Hill on the first attempt, and when Dad tried to gear down, the engine would stall so that he had to back down to the bottom of the hill and try another run at it. Unfortunately, the car usually broke down just as we had negotiated the corner above the canal, and Dad was not skilled at backing. Another drawback with the Jowett, and other cars of the era, was the fact that they had to be 'cranked up' in order to start the engine. A metal crank was supplied, which Dad inserted through a hole in the front of the car, after which he jerked it round and round until the engine 'caught'. This took a lot of strength, and Dad would be gasping before we even got ourselves on the road.

Our immediate family of three eventually became one of four when brother Peter was born in 1932. I was sent to stay with my Granny Wallis on that occasion and came back to find a usurper installed along with a witchlike old lady named Mrs Sparham (pronounced Sparram), who was to look after Mam during the mandatory ten days she was expected to stay in bed after giving birth. Mrs Sparham came from Heage where, Dad claimed, 'they hang 'em in bunches'. (I'm not sure how the village earned this description—perhaps the inhabitants were once a trifle rough?) In any case, Mrs Sparham was certainly an odd old lady with her black clothes and bonnet, like a character out of Dickens. It also turned out that she had the strangest ideas about baby care. 'If you want to keep 'im quiet, Mrs Wallis,' she confided one day, 'put a bit of rum in 'is bottle'.

I was, of course, jealous of the newcomer, and one evening after Mam had bathed brother Peter in a basin by the fire and he was sitting on her knee, I went over and bit his toe. I remember feeling a mixed wave of both love and hate as I did so. Peter, naturally, howled the house down, and Dad put me over the end of the sofa and spanked my bottom hard. It is the one spanking I remember.

CHAPTER 3

Dad

Ted, Arnold, and Jack Wallis

MY PARENTS WERE MARRIED in Old Matlock Parish Church on August 13 1927, their honeymoon spent in the company of my Aunt Flo, aged seventeen, in Newton-Stewart, Wigtonshire, Scotland. Aunt Flo's mother, my Granny, had pointed out that her daughter 'needed a holiday' and should go on the honeymoon too, and apparently my father had not demurred. Nevertheless, I was born nine months later. (My mother never put her reaction into words, but the roll of her eyes when years later she told me the story said it all.)

As a young boy of twelve or so, having no radio or television to ensnare him like many children of his time, Dad wrote stories and poems. His subjects tended to be pirates, or characters with names such as Desperate Dan. These stories came out as occasional 'papers' which he later made into small books, sewing the pages together and fixing some sort of Rexene material to their covers. He called these volumes *Our Boys* and modelled them on *The Boy's Own Paper* to which he and his brother Arnold had a subscription. Often, the stories ended as a literal cliffhanger with the words 'To be continued', plus a drawing of the hero clinging to the face of a precipice. Now and again readers were warned that a story such as *Treasure Trove* 'will probably end soon', but to 'Look out next month for *The Black Knight: A Tale of the Days of Chivalry*'. A drawing of the knight mounted on a rearing horse and flourishing a sword would accompany this. Other stories seem to have disappeared altogether: 'These school series which take up so much room will have to be abandoned for a while, and *The Midnight Mail*, by J.W., will start next month in its place', my father informed his readers. The books were copiously illustrated with drawings in pencil or ink with a few watercolours here and there. F. Calvert and Paul Hardy, friends of Dad's who also lived in Ambergate, supplied one or two of the drawings. Dad wrote poems, too, and one of his verses became a family joke: 'The snow/Gives to the woods a pretty mantle/While on the fire/The bacon fries'. It was almost haiku. Granddad would often quote the poem, adding, 'Your Dad was always thinking of his food!'

Also like *The Boys' Own Paper*, there were riddles in the little books and prizes offered for the first correct answer. An A. Wallis often won the prizes, not surprisingly since Dad's younger brother was one of only three or four readers. Prizes offered would be described, rather mysteriously, as 'a coloured plate', 'a strong O.B. book shelf', or 'a bracket'. How to do conjuring tricks was also described in the books, along with instructions on how to care for a lizard, or a cavy (rabbit), complete with drawings of how to construct their home—in the latter case, the animal's caviary. There was also a page headed 'Wit, Fun and Mirth', which contained such gems as, 'Master to dull boy, "If it were not for me you'd be the biggest blockhead on earth!"' and, 'It seems absurd to speak of a blind man's favourite colour, but we've all heard of blind man's buff'. Finally, in the October edition of *Our Boys*, the editor noted, 'In 1915 we are thinking of starting a new magazine for boys called *The Boy's Own Magazine*. But we have not decided yet'.

After leaving school at the age of fourteen, Dad worked for a while as office boy in the General Stores Department of the Midland Railway as many lower middle class boys did then. He was eighteen when he was called up and joined the Royal Navy in 1918, the year the war ended. There, he was trained as a wireless operator on a battleship and witnessed his first and only casualty of war when an unfortunate sailor blew his own hand off with one of the ship's guns. The photo of my father shows him looking extraordinarily young in his Royal Navy uniform with the sailor's bell-bottomed trousers, a shirt with a large, square collar, and a small round cap. I still have his black silk Royal Navy scarf.

Jack Wallis in his Royal Navy uniform

Physically, Dad was quite tall for an Englishman of that era, about five feet eleven, with thin, dark hair, a big hooked nose, and large brown eyes. His ears stuck out from his head, rather like those of Bing Crosby, the crooner who was to be popular in the forties.

About the time of his marriage in 1927, after a post-war stint as a navvy digging ditches on Hartsay Hill, Dad took a job as a commercial traveller working for General Refractories, Ltd, a company that made bricks and furnace linings.

The late twenties and early thirties must have been a difficult time for my parents, although I was unaware of it at the time. The Depression was beginning, and this was my father's first real job. Eventually, he made a success of his occupation as a commercial traveller, although anyone less like the Willy Loman type associated with such work must be rare as a masticating hen. In my early childhood I would see him sitting, ankles crossed, in our tiny back room, his attaché case over his knees in lieu of a desk, writing out the day's report with a fountain pen. He always used green ink and wrote with what seemed to me a flourish. As a rule, he wore hairy tweed plus fours and shapeless jackets, the pockets of which he crammed with pens, notebooks, and voluminous handkerchiefs until they sagged like saddlebags. He kept his shoes highly polished.

Dad was a smoker, and had a pipe that he tapped against the back of the fireplace in order to dislodge its 'dottle'. He also smoked cigarettes, usually Player's, which had a picture of a sailor on the package. He aspired to be a bit of a dandy, I think now, and

Jack Wallis (Dad)

up-to-the-minute, hence the plus fours and the green ink. As a father, he was at times a jovial friend, at other times remote and not to be disturbed. In those days, the women ruled the roost at home, with their men's permission, while it was assumed that the men were fully engaged in bringing home the bacon. The mothers brought up the children, with only an occasional input from the fathers in the form of a spanking. 'Wait 'til your Dad gets home,' was a frequent cry up and down our row of houses. But Dad was a loving father, and I remember only the one severe spanking I received: the one after I had chomped down on Peter's toe.

As a child I found my father much more fun than my mother—unfairly because she had to be the martinet while Dad could be our pal. He retained a certain *Boy's Own Paper* type of youthfulness all his life, and at times would let his hair down to tease and joke with us. However, he never read us stories or played any games other than to occasionally take the role of bowler in our games of cricket at the seaside. From time to time, he took us on walks, usually to visit our Wallis grandparents, or drove us over to Beeley or Stanton moor for a picnic. He also liked to show us games he and Arnold had played as boys. One evening he asked Mam for a candle, lit it, doused the electric light, and showed us how to make dogs and butterflies with hand shadows on the living room wall.

On one memorable occasion, he and I took a walk through the fields to where he promised he would show me a fairy ring (I believed in fairies at the time). As he told me about it, I looked at Dad's face carefully to make sure he wasn't teasing, but there wasn't a glimmer of a smile, so I trustingly took his hand and we set off. By the time we arrived at the field where the promised ring lay, I, bubbling inside with anticipation, leapt into the middle of it, closed my eyes, held out my arms, twirled about in the approved fashion, and asked the fairies for…I have forgotten what I demanded of the fairies, but for me the whole episode was magic. When I was much older, Dad told me the fairy ring had been the circle formed when a farmer left a wheel of his farm cart lying among the grasses at the side of his field; nonetheless, I still remember the magic of that moment.

Although a slender man, Dad was very fond of his food. He loved all manner of sweet things, and savouries such as various cheeses, herrings soused in vinegar and capers, and roast meats of all kinds. He loved toast spread with beef dripping, the fat that comes from the meat when it is roasted (we found it delicious, and hadn't yet heard of cholesterol). At breakfast, he demanded his bacon be what he called crozzled, that is, very crisp. (In Margaret Drabble's *The Peppered Moth*, I discovered that crozzle is the name used for a by-product in the production of steel. It looks rather like over-fried bacon.) He particularly liked a kind of meat and vegetable spread that Mam made by mincing together the remains of the stew. He called it frummety, although perhaps he was thinking of furmenty, a very different, sweet, medieval dish. Despite his slender build, Dad was, as Grandfather insisted, 'a good trencherman'.

Dad often wore 'flannel bags', trousers of grey wool, which he pinched at the knee and hoisted up a little as he sat down in an effort to preserve their crease. At night, he put special trousers into a trouser press, an oblong contraption with a hinged top and bottom between which he clamped the trouser legs with their creases aligned, the two sides held together with screws. In the morning, the theory went, the trousers would look as if they had been ironed. Dad's plus fours were usually of tweed and had a strap and buckle just below knee level where he secured the pants at the top of his knee-high socks. These, and plus twos, a slimmer version, may be seen on golfers today; they are still very popular in Scotland both for golfing and for striding over (usually wet) moors. With his grey woollen trousers or his plus fours, Dad wore a shirt, a tie and a jacket, tweed in winter and linen in summer. He had one summer jacket that Mam said made him look as though he should have been selling ice cream.

When they went out, like most men Dad wore a Trilby hat—a felt fedora with a narrow brim, which it was *de rigueur* to raise to women of his acquaintance on the street. For motoring, he wore a flat cap and 'driving gloves': gauntlets with huge cuffs that came to his mid-forearm. In the thirties, when a man and woman were walking together, it was customary for the man to offer the woman his arm and to walk on the outside of the pavement. Perhaps this arose when women wore long dresses that might be splashed by passing vehicles, or in earlier times, so that the man could keep his sword arm away from the obstruction of a wall.

Before he reached puberty, brother Pete wore short pants to his knee until, at fourteen, he was 'britched', that is, began to wear long pants or breeches. With shorts, and later, trousers, he had knee socks with stripes round the tops, plus a sweater, shirt, and jacket. (When brother Gib, born in 1940, was britched, Pete and I tormented him by chanting, 'Have no fear/Gibby Long Trousers is here!') Like other young boys in our village, Gib often wore boots with 'seggs' which helped their shoe soles last longer. The boots looked enormous at the ends of his spindly little boy legs.

CHAPTER 4
The Durwards

Alice 'Sizme' Durward

MY MOTHER'S DURWARD FAMILY lived in Matlock, which at the time was famous for its hydros—today we would call them spas—where the sick came to take soothing baths and be slapped and pummelled back to health. Early in the century, there were twenty or more hydros in the town, but by the time I came on the scene, there were only three, including the largest and earliest that had been built in 1886 by John Smedley of cotton fame. Smedley charged visitors two guineas a week, forbade alcohol and card playing, and allowed only sacred music.

Matlock was not a big industrial town, although it did have sand and limestone quarries from which we heard explosions from time to time and from which lorries emerged, carrying rocks of lime or gritstone destined for builders up and down the country.

By the standards of the thirties, the Durward family was considered lower class. They all spoke with a Derbyshire accent, using many of the wonderful expressions I would come across again at Fritchley School. For each member of the family, the dialect was weaker, or stronger, depending on with whom he or she associated. Working men, such as Uncle Bud who was a farmer, had a stronger dialect than that of my mother, whose speech had been modified by her association with Dad; Uncles Reg and George, who worked at local hydros, heard more cultivated accents during the day, and this probably affected their own speech to some degree. My grandparents spoke in the strongest dialects of all.

In her young married days, I suspect my mother was very lonely for her large family in Matlock. In any event, we would visit my grandmother at least once a week, and she would visit us, often with my Uncle Jack in tow. He was only eleven to my five or so, and we played together. He often took me to the nearby Cromford Canal to fish for tadpoles. Mam would give me a jam jar with a string handle, along with a small butterfly net she had bought from Woolworth's in Belper, so that we could fish under the little bridge, putting the hapless tadpoles into the jar along with water dipped from the canal and a little 'waterweed' for them to swim among. I was not allowed to keep them in the house and remember them becoming frogs on only one occasion. I suspect Mam threw them out as soon as I seemed to have lost interest. Once, when Jack and I were kneeling on the flagstones under the canal bridge, dipping for tadpoles, two unknown boys came by and threatened us. I wept, but Jack said 'Mardy! What are you crying for?' and drove the boys away. I was very impressed.

Granny Durward particularly enjoyed her visits to us in spring when the bluebells were in bloom, an azure carpet that covered the floor of the woods bordering the canal and those of Hurt's Shining Cliff across the river. In those days we were not restrained by the knowledge that bluebells, or any other flower, could become extinct. Granny would gather armfuls of the blossoms to take home to Matlock; it was not unusual for her to fill a bucket with them. The only rule we gave ourselves on these flower expeditions was that we should snap off each stalk cleanly and not pull it so that the white part came away, which we believed would kill the bulb. A little later, cowslips, a member of the primrose family, came into bloom in the fields, and we would gather bouquets to take home.

The thirties was certainly a time of ecological incorrectness. Little boys often made collections of wild birds' eggs; my brother Peter had such a collection, as had Dad as a boy. The rule was that only one egg was to be taken from a nest, although no thought was given to the fact that if several small boys went bird-nesting (bod-nestin' in local parlance), the unfortunate mother bird could be left with no young. Pete would bring his eggs home, prick a small hole at either end, gently blow out the contents, and afterwards glue the shells to a board and carefully label them. Even though we girls usually didn't collect eggs, we nevertheless searched the hedges for bird's nests so that we could have the thrill of peeking in at the mother bird sitting on her eggs. When bod-nestin' at Fritchley, the rule was: 'Yo munna frayten 'er' (You mustn't frighten her).

Also in the 1930s we had never heard of, or even thought, about recycling. Everything was dumped into the dustbin to be emptied by the local authority every week. Fortunately, we had little plastic except cellophane and the Bakelite from which our telephones were made; food we bought at the shops was packed in paper bags, which Mam saved for wrapping sandwiches when we went to the moors for a picnic. Our newspapers had few pages, and these were reserved for starting our kitchen fire in the morning.

Our weekly trips to Matlock to see the Durward family began with my proudly donning a red woollen coat with trousers to match. To keep the trousers snug against my legs, there was elastic across their cuffs to pull under the instep of my shoes. Mam and I then walked hand-in-hand to Ambergate station, which in the 1930s still had six platforms, including an 'up' and a 'down' for the Sheffield line to the north east, and another two that went northwest to and from Manchester. The station, being a junction, was built as a triangle with two platforms on either side of each set of rails. The third side of the triangle was the means of transferring goods wagons from the Sheffield to the Manchester line, and vice versa.

Mam and I took a Manchester train, waiting for it on a platform across the lines from the only one left today. It had a waiting room, plus an exciting machine that, if you inserted a penny, would disgorge a small bar of chocolate. I was sometimes able to persuade Mam to part with a penny, especially if the train were late.

The arrival of the train always made me shudder. The locomotive was huge and black, with two great iron wheels on either side between which the pistons moved up and down, hissing steam. On top of the forward cabin sat a chimney and a bowl-shaped whistle. Unlike the thrilling *woo-woooo* of an American locomotive's hooter, this made a shriek such as the legendary lady might make when spotting a mouse. A fire in the cabin produced the steam, and it was the fireman's job to shovel coal from the tender behind the locomotive onto the fire, while the engine driver kept his hand on the throttle and an eye out for signals. The guard's van was attached to the back of the train and was where the guard took care of packages, bicycles, and the odd cage of homing pigeons. The pigeons were a hobby, mostly of coal miners. They kept their birds in lofts in their backyards, and whenever they wanted to test their pets' homing instincts, they arranged with fellow enthusiasts in another part of the country to receive their crated birds at a station maybe fifty miles away, released them, and sent the empty cages back by train. I've wondered since if this hobby was popular with miners because they themselves spent so much time cooped up underground that it gave them a feeling of release to have their pets fly free for the journey home.

When we stopped at the stations, I watched the guard alight to deliver any crates and parcels to the stationmaster's office and help passengers open and close the heavy carriage doors that had handles only on the outside. To open the doors from inside, the passengers had to let down the window in the door using a wide leather strap and then lean out to reach the handle. Finally, with a toot on his whistle and a wave of his flag, the guard signalled the engine driver to leave.

Each compartment was the width of the train with long, padded seats on each side and mirrors or pictures of the countryside above them. Above those were the net luggage racks. There was no corridor, toilet facilities, or any means of walking the length of the train; once in your compartment, you had to stay there until you arrived at the next station.

For me, the journey to Matlock was full of interest, particularly when we passed our row of houses and I was able to look into our neighbours' windows and into the gardens to see who was playing with whom. The next station was Whatstandwell with its well-tended garden full of daffodils and tulips in the spring and delphiniums, marguerites, and phlox in the summer. Ambergate station had no garden, but most of the others did so, and a prize was offered each year for the best. Whatstandwell and Matlock Bath, further up the line, were often winners. Each of these smaller stations had its stationmaster, and a porter who was usually waiting for the train with his parcels or pigeon boxes piled onto a long, flat barrow. Both men wore black or navy uniforms with the addition of a flat, army-style cap for the stationmaster. Another thrill for me was when we approached Matlock and the train ran through the long, dark tunnels that pierced the limestone cliffs of High Tor.

At Matlock station, Mam and I crossed the lines by way of a glass-enclosed bridge to near the present-day bookstall. Sir Joseph Paxton, the architect who designed St Pancras station in London, and the rock gardens, glass houses, and Edensor village on the Chatsworth estate, was also the architect for Matlock station. Once over the river bridge, Mam and I walked up Bank Road to

Granny's house at 2 (now 18) St John's Terrace, Wellington Street. This was an extremely steep climb that easily reached an angle of one in seven towards the top. Sometimes, Mam would splurge a few pennies, and we'd take a bus and ride to the top of the hill by way of Steep Turnpike, leave the bus near the Duke of Wellington, a pub about a quarter mile above Granny's house, and walk down.

In the 1920s there was a tram for visitors to the hydros that was hauled up Bank Road by a steel cable wound around a huge drum at the top of the hill near Rockside Hydro. (Rockside has recently been refurbished into flats.) As one tram was hauled up, another one, to balance it, was lowered down the hill to Crown Square: tuppence up, a penny down. I distinctly remember the thrill of travelling up Bank Road on this tram; however, some years ago in a book about the history of Matlock, I learned that the tram was discontinued in 1927, the year before I was born. (As I said earlier, I was a romantically inclined child.) The small gazebo that now sits under its clock tower at the northern end of the Hall Leys Park used to be in the centre of Crown Square and acted as a station for the trams. Earlier still, it had been the collecting point for the broughams Granddad drove when he delivered customers to Smedley's Hydro.

To me, Grandmother Durward's house was exciting: full of the smells of Mansion Polish, black-leading, and baking bread. Black-leading was the paste containing graphite that Granny rubbed onto her fireplace hood and its surrounds in order to make them shine. The house was part of a row of about ten tall four-story houses, each attached to the next by a common wall.

They were built in the 1800s to house those who worked at the hydros. They sat on a steep hillside and were built of local sandstone. Worn stone steps led down from the living quarters to the coal cellar and a laundry room, the latter equipped, as was our scullery, with a zinc tub, a 'poncher' used to agitate the dirty laundry, and a gas water heater. The room also doubled as a bathroom, and filling the low, zinc bath with hot water was hard work, which was probably why members of the family bathed only once a week. The tub was pulled close to the basement fire, with a fireguard around the room side of the tub and a sheet draped over it for privacy and added warmth.

The basement, which had a window that looked over the town to Masson Hill, afforded the sort of view for which visitors to Smedley's Hydro further down Bank Road would pay through the nose. Later, there would be a bathroom with a lavatory on this floor, but back in the thirties, one had to exit the back door and walk down the garden and more steps to an alley that ran behind the houses. There, a row of low buildings was the site of the earth closets, one per house; for the residents of St John's Terrace; going to the toilet was not a private affair. For toilet paper, Granny would ask Uncle Bud to bore a hole through the flimsy pages of an old telephone directory so that she could thread a string through it and hang it on a nail hammered into the privy wall. For our night time needs, every bed had its chamber pot. At the rear of the basement, on the Wellington Street side and up three steps, was the coal cellar with a grate in the ceiling that opened onto the little concrete area beyond the front door. Here, every couple of months, the coalman would tip into it Granny's order of so many hundredweights of coal.

Up the worn stone steps from the basement was the kitchen that also overlooked the lovely view of the town and the nearby hills. There was a sink in one corner with a tap for cold water and a gas copper above it for hot. It also had a fireplace with a side oven and a mantelshelf above it. Granny's old sofa sat under the window, and there was a sideboard, a corner cupboard for cups and plates, and a large kitchen table with four chairs in the middle of the room.

The other room on this floor was the gloomy sitting room, complete with the usual Victorian roll-ended sofa and a couple of easy chairs. It was seldom used, and during the war Granny rented it out to an old man, a refugee from the London bombing. The windows on this side of the house overlooked St John's Terrace and were always shadowed by the shop and the bakery on the opposite hillside. Above the sitting room were two more bedrooms and above those the attic where my grandfather slept. Gas lamps on wall brackets in each room and on the landing lighted the house. In the back living room/kitchen, the gaslight hung from the ceiling in the middle of the room. Each light had a mantel, a small, thimble-shaped piece of what looked like starched fabric that was very fragile and broke with the touch of a finger. To light the mantel, Granny pulled a small chain to release the gas, which she lit with a match.

The windows overlooked the steep little garden with its purple lilac tree and Granny's 'pianas' (peonies). There was also a wide view of Starkholmes, Masson Hill, and Riber Castle that John Smedley had built as his residence in 1863. It was complete with battlements and sat on top of a hill overlooking the town. The locals dubbed it Smedley's Folly because at first it had been difficult to get water up to it. Since Smedley's time, the castle has housed a boy's school, a store for the Ministry of Defence during World War II, and most recently a zoo. Today, the new owners have been given permission to convert the now derelict castle and its outbuildings into apartments.

Granny's house was busy, and there were always uncles coming in or neighbours visiting. Without bothering to knock, they would enter through the front door and walk down the long corridor to the kitchen on the other side of the house. The corridor had a row of hooks along it where the family hung their work clothes and coats; it held a strong smell of sweat. When a family member or a neighbour appeared at the kitchen door, Granny would exclaim, 'Eeh! I say!', her eyes wide as though the visit had taken her by surprise.

Uncle Bud, who was still living at home, often left his lorry on the street and came in to have dinner with us. Bud was tall, craggy-faced, and very fair, his eyes a bright blue. Because of his colouring, the family nicknamed him 'the Swede', and in view of the fact that the area was once within the Dane-geld, it is very likely that he and the rest of the family has some Viking blood. And there was Jack, also coming home from school for midday dinner, to play with me or spend the hour in teasing. In the thirties, dinner was served in the middle of the day in the northern counties, as it still is on farms. The evening meal, called tea, was often something fried: fish, or sausages with a scrambled egg. Lunch, or luncheon, was upper class and therefore posh and anathema.

When we visited, Mam usually helped Granny by kneading a batch of bread that she baked in the side oven. The oven had to be 'got used to' because there was no way to regulate it. On bread-making days, the fire in the black-leaded grate would be built up so that the little kitchen was overpoweringly hot. Granny then judged when the oven was ready by opening its door and putting her hand inside; I don't remember that she ever made a mistake. When the loaves came from the oven, Granny rapped them sharply on the undersides, listening for a hollow sound; she and Mam always knew when the bread 'sounded done'. If not, the loaves were returned to the oven for another few minutes. One day, when Mam was busy at the table kneading dough, she said to her mother, 'Fancy, Mam, I'm thirty!' It was as though she couldn't believe she had reached such an enormous age. I, eight at the time, couldn't believe it, either.

After the bread came from the oven, Mam and Granny would have a cup of tea and a slice of the new bread slathered with butter. There was usually a small argument over who should have the crust: 'You 'ave it, our Cis.' 'No, you, Mam.' We all thought the crust was the best part of the loaf. If her tea were too hot, Granny always poured a little into her saucer and blew on it until it was cool enough to drink—from the saucer. Many of the older working-class people cooled and drank their tea in this way, but Mam would not allow me to do this; it was 'all right for Granny', but not, apparently, for me.

While Mam was busy with her baking, I often spent the time making drawings to go into my scrapbooks. Unfortunately, I had little to hold them in place. Scotch tape (we called it sticky tape) had been invented in 1930, but neither my mother nor the Ambergate shopkeepers had yet become aware of it. Sometimes Mam mixed up a flour paste for me, but unless I took care, it soaked through the paper and ruined my drawings. Most weeks, I waited until I was home to ask my father for some 'stamp edging', which I peeled from his sheet of stamps, licked, and used as a fixative for my artwork. It was a clumsy expedient, but better than nothing. Also in Matlock, in order to label my drawings, I would put up a hue and cry for 'the pencil'. There was seldom more than one available, and it usually needed sharpening. Granny did this for me with a paring knife, because the only sharpener available was a tiny, hand-held one that did an inferior job. A pen was out of the question because Mam had declared them 'messy'. Pens consisted of a wooden shaft with a metal nib on the end that had to be dipped into a bottle of ink, often leading to blots. There were no ballpoints or Biros then.

One of Mam's biggest problems during the week was keeping in touch with Granny. We had a phone at Number 5, one of the few in the village (our number was Ambergate 65), but we had it only because Dad needed to keep in touch with his customers. Neither Granny nor any of our relatives had phones, so we were unable to speak to them directly. Very occasionally, if

Mam had an urgent message for my grandmother in Matlock, she phoned a local shop opposite Granny's house to ask that a message be taken to her. Otherwise, we had to either catch a train to Matlock, or write a letter, which could take a couple of days to be delivered, despite the fact that letters were delivered twice a day. Letters cost a penny each to send when I was quite small; later they went up to tuppence ha'penny. If we had an extremely urgent message, we could have sent a telegram, but both Mam and Granny considered this to be overdoing things.

Granny Durward was a small woman, and rather bent even in her youth. She had dark hair that she curled with a ferocious-looking curling iron that she heated up in a gas flame. There was often a smell of singeing hair at Matlock. At night, Granny often walked down Bank Road with us to the station. Usually the lamplighter was busy then, lighting the gas lamps that still illuminated Matlock's streets at night. We had electric streetlights in Ambergate, but in Matlock the change to electric power in streets and houses was not complete until after the Second World War.

Our weekly trips to Matlock always included a visit, Mam's oldest and probably her only friend. Mam made no others in her life; her large family was sufficient for her. She made only acquaintances among the young mothers of Matlock Road, and usually called them by their married names: Mrs Gratrix, Mrs Hurst, Mrs Chisnell. Only once, in an emergency, did I hear her call Mrs Gratrix 'Bertha'. In Fritchley it was Mrs Rollinson or Mrs Howiss, although those two neighbour women called one another by their first names. However, with Auntie Jess it was different. They had been friends since their early youth, had attended local dances together, and played tennis in the Hall Leys Park. A snap of them was taken around 1925, both women dressed in long and shapeless 'tennis frocks' and wielding the oddly shaped tennis racquets of the day.

Mam with Jess Ballington

Jess was small, stooped, and dark-haired when I first knew her and looked very much older than Mam. She lived in a little house with a large garden just below Granny Durward's house. Because of the steepness of the hillside, all we could see of the Ballington house from my grandmother's window was its roof and back wall, with an occasional glimpse of Jess nipping to the coal shed at the back of the house for a scuttle of coal. I was fond of Aunt Jess and enjoyed visiting her house, which was very old, probably sixteenth century, and full of polished brass ornaments, very like the houses in my illustrated storybooks. The Ballingtons were gardeners and sold plants and produce in a shop near Crown Square.

Sometime in the 1930s, Granny Durward took a job. Times were hard, and Granddad's wages minimal, as were Uncle Bud's, who was still driving the milk lorry and living at home. Whatever the reason, Granny began working as a cleaner at the Bank of Scotland that sat across the river bridge near the foot of Bank Road. She had to be there before the bank opened, which meant that six mornings a week she would rise early, curl her hair with her curling iron, put on her best, and only, coat and hat, and sidestep down to Crown Square. She sidestepped, both because of the steepness of the hill and because it was paved with uneven gritstone bricks down most of its length. Her heels would catch in the cracks of the pavement so that sidestepping was the only way she could keep on her feet. Family lore has it that during snowy weather, Granny sometimes negotiated the steep Bank Road on her bottom. No matter how she had arrived at the bank, after two or three hours of tidying up and scrubbing floors, she would reverse her journey and walk up Bank Road again to begin her chores at 2, St John's Terrace.

The seven Durward children

Alice 'Cis' Wallis (Mam)

Uncle Reg

Uncle Eric

Uncle George

Uncle Bud

Aunt Gladys

Uncle Jack

The Durwards, at least the children and their mother, were a close-knit family. I expect there were some tiffs, but for the most part, the children were friends and supported one another even into old age. I remember only one violent argument: Uncle Reg, a small, banty-cock of a man, his dark hair sleeked back, is standing before the fireplace in Granny Durward's kitchen. Uncles George and Bud are also there. Uncle George is a small, dark man, although not as solidly built as Uncle Reg. 'The hell with the king!' Reg declared, his fists curled, 'I'm off to join the Black Shirts!' These were fascist storm troopers headed by a man named Mosley, an admirer of Hitler. Granny was both astonished and afraid. 'Our Reg, that's treason!' she cried. Bud and George loudly agreed, and Reg walked out in a huff. But Uncle Reg was no fascist, and certainly didn't join the Black Shirts. He had been a member of the Royal Army Medical Corps since at least 1931, and a few years after this episode, he was at Dunkirk fighting for King and country, carrying our wounded soldiers from the beach to the small boats that had come across the Channel to take them back to Britain.

In my childhood, Grandfather Durward seemed to me to be an outcast and, feeling sorry for him, I always greeted him when he came home for dinner. We would hear him coming, breathing heavily up the stairs from the cellar, having entered the house by the rear door. As he opened the kitchen door, he would gasp 'Oh, pee op!' We never knew what it meant, but he always said it when he entered, or when he seated himself in his chair near the fireplace. Only my grandmother would greet him, 'Hello,

Griff', and take his meal from the oven where she had placed it to keep warm. Everyone else ignored him and went on with whatever they had been doing. Because I felt sorry for him, I would say, 'Hello, Granddad!' But he would look at me without reply, and only grunt. One day, however, after I had given him my usual hello, Grandfather handed me a small 'golliwog' pin shaped like the little black figure that appeared on the side of jars of Chivers marmalade or in their advertisements. (Today we would consider such a pin racist.) He had found the brooch when emptying one of that day's dustbins. The next week, proudly conscious of the new brooch on the collar of my dress and full of hope, I again greeted my grandfather, 'Hello, Granddad'. Grandfather only grunted.

I learned later that my grandfather used to beat my grandmother and his sons, never the girls, until one of the boys became old enough and large enough to challenge him. Much later, I wondered what psychological damage had been caused, to my grandmother, my uncles, my aunt, and my mother, having this sort of violence in the house. At least it explained why the family never spoke to him.

CHAPTER 5

Mam

Mam at 2, St John's Terrace, Matlock

ALICE (CISSIE) DURWARD, BORN in Darley Dale in 1906, was a short, pretty woman with a large mouth (generous, she called it), very blue eyes, and a lot of fair, curly hair. I called her Mam because that was what members of the working class called their mothers; she would have found Mummy too swanky. According to family legend, Mam was 'a bit of a lass' when young, and I was told that when she met my father and his current girlfriend at a dance in a nearby village, she 'ran her off'. That is, she took over.

My mother was a housewife, as all married women were expected to be, except when the family coffers were empty. When young, she never worked outside her home, but instead had taken on, or more likely had thrust upon her, the usual job of the eldest girl in a large working-class family: helping to raise the younger children. Mam's impoverished class produced two types of homemaker: those, like my mother, who were meticulous, their children neatly dressed, and those who lived amidst dirt and acrimony, their offspring in rags and with noses dripping copiously.

My most vivid early memory of my mother was on a Monday when the little scullery was filled with steam from the boiling copper and the floor awash with soapsuds. Monday in the '30s was always washday. Mam had a dolly tub, a zinc vessel about four feet tall into which she poured buckets of hot water from the boiler and added soap flakes (no detergents yet), followed by the dirty washing. She then swirled the clothes round in the tub with a poncher like the one at Matlock. This had a long handle like that of a broom, a metal addition that looked like a colander attached to the business end, and two pegs at the top that formed the handle. Mam would seize these handles and vigorously swirl the poncher back and forth among the clothing, rather in the way the agitator in a clothes washer does today.

Mother boiled the dirtier clothes in the boiler, a large, round copper tank, heated by a gas flame, that stood in a corner of the scullery. She transferred the boiled clothes to the dolly with a wooden 'copper stick', a rather hazardous operation during which she shouted at me to stand back if I came too near. When the time came for rinsing, she added a little cloth bag to the dolly tub that contained a hard substance called 'bluing', which put a faint blue cast on the washing and made white clothes appear whiter, rather in the way old ladies had their white hair blued in the 1960s and '70s.

After the boiling, ponching, and rinsing came the mangling. The mangle folded down to become the scullery table for the rest of the week, but on Mondays Mam raised the tabletop and hauled the mangle's innards into an upright position. Then, again with the copper stick, she hoisted sheets, underwear, and towels one by one from the dolly into a bucket and from there to the mangle where she fed them through the wooden rollers that revolved as she vigorously turned the handle. The whole operation was hard, hot, and desperately exhausting; like old age, washday was not for the faint-hearted. On fine days, hanging out the laundry on the line that stretched between two wooden posts alongside the garden path must have been a welcome opportunity to get outdoors into the sunshine. In wet weather, sheets, nappies, and other washing hung dankly about the house for days. No wonder we changed our underclothes only once a week.

My mother's allocation of her weekly jobs, 'me routine', she called it, began with this Monday washing ritual, as was true of the other housewives on Matlock Road. Tuesday was ironing day, and Mam ironed everything, even the tea towels and sheets, afterwards 'airing' anything that was to be worn or slept on. She did this by draping the sheets, underwear, shirts, and blouses over the fireguard.

Until the forties, when my mother brought home an electric iron, getting one's clothes wrinkle-free was a chancy business. Her first iron was not electric, but one she heated on a trivet over the fire. This meant that by the time the iron was ready, its bottom was often covered in soot and Mam had to wipe it off before she could use it, or else it was too hot, and she had to be careful not to scorch the fabric. Later, after we had moved to Fritchley, she had not only an electric iron, but also an airing cupboard built around the hot water tank where she placed the ironed items. Everything had to be thoroughly aired, otherwise Mam was sure that we would all come down with pneumonia, and maybe rheumatism as well.

Cooking was also primitive. At first, the only oven my mother had at Ambergate was the one attached to the fireplace in the dining/family room. On baking days, or when she was cooking a roast or making bread, Mam built up the fire early because it would take a couple of hours for the oven to become hot enough. This was fine in winter, but in summer it made the little room unbearably warm. Hot water for washing and bathing was also heated by the fire, and on baking days the hot water tank in a cupboard in the upstairs bedroom could be heard rumbling ominously as the water boiled.

A year or so before we moved to Ballantrae House in 1937, Mam acquired a gas stove and thus more control over the heat of her oven. Before the gas stove, she cooked all vegetables and jams on a trivet over the fire. The trivet, a little moveable shelf, pivoted so that it could be swung away from the flames when the food was cooked.

Wednesday was the day Mam 'cleaned through'. Everything had to be cleaned. First of all, she swept any carpets with a Ewebank sweeper, a hand-driven contraption with a rotating brush that she ran back and forth over the carpet. It had a pan in front of the brush that, when full, could be emptied onto the garden. No one I knew owned a vacuum cleaner. On special occasions, my mother took the smaller rugs out into the garden where she threw them over the washing line and beat them with a carpet beater, a long-handled piece of equipment with a flat, blade-like end. After this she brushed the stairs. These were carpeted, with stair rods across the bottoms of the risers to hold the carpet in place. Mam would take a stiff-bristled brush and a dustpan for this job, brushing the dust and soil into the pan as she backed down the stairs. She then polished the wood on either side of the stair carpet and mopped the linoleum in the little back room and the wooden floors of the sitting room, after which she polished any lino with red Mansion Polish.

The scullery floor would need only 'a lick and a promise' since Mam had already given it a thorough scrubbing on Monday when, if there had been any handy, she would have rubbed sour milk into the tiles to make them shine. I don't remember if there was any smell from this, but the thirties was not an odourless era, and I probably wouldn't have noticed if there had been.

As if this cleaning through were not enough, after a vigorous dusting of the furniture, Mam scrubbed the front doorstep and applied red Mansion Polish to it. This was called holystoning the step, presumably to keep the devil out. Granny Durward, in Matlock, usually went a step further: after holystoning her front step, she would take a bucket of water and 'swill down' the pavement and the street outside her house. In those days, housework was serious business, especially in some working class and petit bourgeois households. Naturally enough, I had to keep out of the way when all this activity was going on. When I was older, I kept out of view in case my assistance was demanded; even so, having learned my mother's lesson thoroughly, today I find myself unable to rest, or to write, or to do anything else when my house is untidy about me.

Thursday was 'Matlock Day' when we visited the market that was set up each week in a field now occupied by a large food store. Here, local farmers and shopkeepers set up their tables and displayed their wares: pots and pans, rolls of wallpaper and other hardware items, fish, fruits and vegetables, children's games, underwear and cheap dresses. The stall keepers were a noisy bunch: 'Come and get 'im 'is kippers, me old luv!' one would cry to the circling customers, 'thruppence 'apn'y a pair.' 'Luvly bananas, just in from Jamaica!' shouted another, and another would hold up a pair of bloomers, ''Ow about a set 'o passion killers, luv? Keep 'im busy, eh?' How the housewives loved it, cackling though pretending to be abashed, exclaiming, 'Eeh, I say!'

The more dubious of the stallholders' repartee went over my head; Mam would never explain, but I loved it. I loved it especially when we visited the market at night before taking the bridge over the river to the station to catch our train home to Ambergate. Then the stalls were lit with hissing gas lamps, and the vendors yelled even louder as they struggled to unload the last of their wares. By then, they had made everything cheaper, the kippers thruppence (three pennies) apiece, the bloomers half price, and the gimcrack offerings from Japan just a ha'penny. Occasionally, Mam might buy me some of the little shells which, when dropped into a glass of water, would magically produce a little paper flower. As we made for the station, the lamplighter would be busy at the gas lamps along the streets, pulling down the little chain to get the gas flowing and igniting the mantle with his long-handled lighter.

On Fridays, if Granny Durward and Jack were not visiting, Mam and I often took the green Robin Hood bus to Belper in order to visit Woolworth's 'emporium' with its worn and clattering wooden floor, for a reel of cotton or a skein of silk, the wool shop for wool so Mam could knit another little romper suit for the new baby she was expecting, and Tomes's, the ironmonger on Bridge Street, perhaps for a new hearth brush. On Saturdays, Mam and I stayed home while she prepared the potatoes and vegetables for midday dinner, and, as did all the other local housewives, changed early into her obligatory 'afternoon frock'. For Mam, Saturday was a comparatively restful day.

Every day, of course, she had our meals to prepare. Our diet throughout the Depression was simple. Beef stew was a frequent dish during the week, fried fish appeared now and then, and occasionally a beef or ham roast accompanied by mashed or roasted potatoes and a green vegetable of some sort: cabbage or Brussels sprouts in the winter and string beans or peas in summer. Salads were sometimes served at teatime, although never as an accompaniment to dinner, and consisted of lettuce, spring onions, cucumber, and tomato, but with no rocket, no spinach, no diced red or yellow peppers, or pine nuts. Dessert was rice pudding or blancmange, with the occasional steamed pudding, or pie and custard. Much of this fare became either scarce or unobtainable after war broke out, and we were reduced to Spam, an egg, and an ounce or two of meat, butter, and cheese every week.

After brother Peter was born, when I was four, our trips to Matlock became less frequent. Mam was busier than ever, probably even more so than modern mothers because she was harassed by the draconian rules of a Doctor Ruby King who insisted that babies be fed every four hours. If they howled in between feeds, they were to be left in their prams and allowed to yell—and drive their mothers mad—until it was time for the next meal.

'Training' also made for a lot of wasted time for mothers. I don't know if it was again one of Dr King's mandates, but Mam spent countless hours holding Peter, two months old, over a chamber pot in a futile effort to reduce the number of napkins she had to wash. 'Swee, swee, swee,' she would urge the baby, making what she meant to be the encouraging sound of urine falling into the chamber pot. Or it was 'Go ah, ah for Mammy,' if she was hoping for something larger. Of course, if Peter obliged it was purely accidental, but he would be praised: 'Good baby! Good little lad!' This kind of lavatory regime continued, so that when we were older and had failed to do the mandatory 'number two' for the day, we were dosed the next morning with syrup of figs, which did the trick, but at the expense of a bellyache.

Of course, when Mam was busy with washday, she wore an old dress and a 'pinny'—a pinafore. At other times, such as when she visited Matlock, she 'dressed up'. Women's clothes in the early thirties, when I first became aware of such things, still tended toward the flapperish. Mam's skirts were below her knees, her waist at hip level, and her stockings, in the days before nylon, were silk if she'd felt rich when she'd bought them at the market, and if not, thick greyish lisle. She held up her stockings with suspenders, an integral part of the whalebone corset, or a suspender belt; younger women used garters.

Later in the decade, Mam's dresses became longer, to mid-calf, and she often had little floating capes attached to the shoulders. Clothes tended to be flat bosomed, and as late as 1937, Aunt Gladys was still wearing a flattening contraption, a sort of reverse brassiere, over her breasts like those that had been popular in the 1920s to produce the fashionable boyish look. Mam's dress shoes had either high, rather stubby heels, or they were low and had a strap that buttoned at the side. Her hats at first were cloche and pulled well down on her marcelled head. Marcelled hair was cut very short with a high semicircle shaved up the back of the neck and waves pinched into it from the central part down either side of the head. To fancy it up, there was sometimes a 'spit curl' on the forehead that was often formed with actual spit on a lock of hair, (one's own spit in the best circles). In the early 1930s, Mam's woollen coat was also mid-calf and fit close to her body.

In winter Mrs Gratrix, Margaret's mother, wore a fox fur over her shoulders, fastened at the front so that its little sharp teeth appeared to be biting the end of its tail. I hated its beady stare and was glad Mam didn't wear fur. Mam always wore gloves and a hat when she went to Matlock; after the cloche went out of fashion, her hats were made of felt and had a brim with coloured feathers or other decorations to one side. On very special occasions, such as weddings, some women were sometimes tempted to emulate Queen Mary and wear a toque.

The earliest outfit I can remember wearing was the outdoor set in red wool with leggings and a matching coat. I used to sit on the floor of the sitting room to put on my leggings 'all by myself'. Getting dressed was a struggle. Later, after I became a pupil at Ambergate School, Mam made dresses for me on her Singer sewing machine. I particularly remember one she made when I was six or seven that had the fashionable little cape attached to its shoulders covering the tops of my arms; I felt very grown up. Mam's dressmaking was a little slapdash, but as a small girl I never noticed. We little girls also wore ankle socks in summer and knee socks in winter along with lace-up shoes that invariably formed blisters on our heels the first week or so after we bought them. We expected to have to 'wear in' shoes when they were new. In wet weather we brought out the Wellington boots, which were chilly to wear and often promoted the chilblains that plagued us in the winter months. In summer we wore strap sandals, and over our clothes a gabardine Mac. Cardigans and sweaters, which we called jumpers or woollies, were mostly hand-knitted. School uniforms came later, with grammar school.

CHAPTER 6

A Young Gardener

GARDENING HAS LONG BEEN a preoccupation of my family. Even Grandmother Durward, who had little money to devote to such things, had her little square of lawn surrounded by her favourite plants and a purple lilac bush. Grandmother Wallis had extensive gardens at the several houses she and Granddad rented throughout their married life, always full of plants for which she could rattle off the Latin names. I have no such skill, but nevertheless soon developed the family love of gardening.

My very earliest memories are two: in the first, I am crawling on the floor of the little back room. There is a fire in the hearth with a tall fireguard round it. The guard, a wide, flat U, is about four feet high and stretches from one side of the fireside tiles to the other. It has bars that are about four inches apart, but it is sufficient to keep me from the fire; however, it isn't enough to keep me from the butter that Mam has placed on the oven step to soften. I reach in and scoop out a finger's worth and eat it with relish. The pleasure I had from the butter and the knowledge that Mam objected to my taking it are part of that memory.

But my more important 'madeleine' moment concerned gardens, and began when Mam dumped me out in the garden near Dad, who was busy digging. Probably Mam was busy too and thought it high time that Dad did his share of baby-minding. He seldom did. Men didn't, in those days; they don't much now, either, although to be fair they do more than their fathers and grandfathers did. Whatever the reason, the memory is of sitting there in the sun (it was again in my pre-walking days), and finding the smell of the soil as irresistible as the butter had been. I scoop it up and eat a small mouthful. I find it delicious.

Maybe this is why I now find the smell of a garden after rain profoundly satisfying. And it was probably this, plus Mam's exasperation when I was 'pestering' her one washday, which started me on my lifelong love of gardens and gardening. In the memory I am about four; the conversation is, of course, approximate.

'Mammy, I've got nothing to do!'

'Why don't you go and make yourself a garden?' she asks.

I wander outside. The soil of the little piece of garden she has pointed out to me, just beyond the coal shed, is hard as rock. My small spade won't even touch it. I drift back into the scullery; Mam is mangling, one hand feeding a sheet through the rollers, the other whirling as she turns the handle. The mangled sheet falls into the wash basket.

'Mammy, I can't dig; it's too hard!'

'Oh, for goodness' sake!'

Mam goes to the coal shed for a fork and, with some annoyance, digs the little piece of garden for me. I examine it.

'What shall I do now?'

'Why don't you get some flowers from Wilmot's field?'

Nowadays, would any mother say that to a four-year-old? Apart from the possibility that the child might stray into the road, wouldn't the mother be concerned that people driving past on the busy A6 might snatch her child away? It is true that dangers of any sort were fewer in thirties-era Derbyshire than they are now: fewer murders, fewer robberies and burglaries, fewer child molestations. We left our doors unlocked.

To me, Wilmot's field seems miles away, beyond the last of the houses—maybe a hundred yards. Heart pounding, I wander out and down the entryway carrying my trowel. I turn left and, creeping close to the wall, walk on the pavement alongside the busy road to Farmer Wilmot's field at the end of our row. I look through the five-barred gate and see that Wilmot's cows are far away, on the hill beyond the railway arches. I open the gate and wander in. The sun is hot on my head. I am wearing a cotton dress, socks, and sandals—little girls did not wear jeans or trousers until after the war—and underneath my dress I have on a vest, a 'liberty bodice' (a sort of flannel undershirt), and knickers. It must be springtime because celandines form a brilliant arc at the side of the field, the earliest of the spring flowers shining golden under the sun. There are also field daisies among the grass, tiny white ones with pink at the tips of the petals. With some difficulty, I dig up a celandine root and a daisy and carry them home. I plant them in my garden. I feel proud and happy, and ready for midday dinner. Mam is still mangling.

CHAPTER 7
The Neighbours

Matlock Road, Ambergate

'THEM NEXT DOOR' WAS a phrase Mam used when mentioning any activity indulged in by our neighbours along Matlock Road. It was a saying she had learned from my grandmother, and it would be followed by a discussion of what those neighbours 'were up to now'. Mam was always a little suspicious of anyone not in her immediate family.

The neighbours were innocuous enough: there was Mr Robinson next door who, like my father, worked as a commercial traveller; another man was the retired headmaster of a local school, and there were several men who worked in offices of some sort:

the County Offices, or those of the LMS (the London, Midland, and Scottish Railway), both of which had their local headquarters in Derby. These men caught the 8.10 train each morning, suited up, Trilby hats at a tilt, and briefcases in hand. Some neighbours in the larger houses across the A6 road also did office work, but most were small businessmen. One owned a petrol station; one was a manager at the wireworks, and another owned a fleet of lorries, one of which he drove himself. The women 'didn't work', as the prevailing lie had it, although one woman, in addition to her domestic duties, taught piano to local children whose parents could afford the fee. My friend, Margaret, was one of those budding pianists, but Mam didn't like the sound of a piano, and I was grateful to be spared both the lessons and what seemed to me the boring practice sessions that would have prevented me from playing in the fields; Margaret spent many a fine summer evening indoors. Later, of course, I was sorry I hadn't had the chance to learn to play an instrument.

Several children who became my friends lived along Matlock Road, and at the age of three, I first became aware of Margaret who lived next door. She was almost a year older than I and considerably larger. She had brown, curly hair and dark blue eyes, one of which fascinated me because it looked to one side as the other looked me squarely in the face. One of our earliest encounters took place one morning at the garden fence. Margaret had apparently been having an exchange with her parents, because she informed me that she was a little bugger, to which I was heard to reply proudly, 'I'm a little bugger, too, aren't I, Margaret?' Later, we spent considerable time attempting to break down the fence between our two gardens so that we could visit one another's houses more quickly. 'Bugger' and 'bloody' were the two verboten swear words of my youth, even though adults often called children 'young buggers' if they were mischievous. I never heard any other terms of abuse, and I was practically an adult before I knew what bugger meant; I suspect that in those days, most of the adults around me didn't know what it meant, either.

Margaret was an only child, her father a clerk who worked for the railway in Derby and went off every morning with his briefcase to catch the 8.10 train. The family was from Manchester, and the parents had strong Lancashire accents: 'Now, think on!' Mrs Gratrix would warn, very Lancastrian, when Margaret seemed about to flout one of her rules.

There was one rough family on Matlock Road; I'll call them the Binnses. They had a young boy, Cyril, who was too old for me to befriend. Mr Binns was a large man—hefty, Mam called him. His wife was smaller, stout and bosomy, and to me seemed to be perpetually angry. One day, when Mam and I were out in the garden, Mr Binns pursued his wife down their garden path, repeatedly slapping and punching her. 'Mrs Wallis! Mrs Wallis, help!' Mrs Binns shrieked, but my mother quickly shepherded me into the house, closed the door, and pretended she hadn't heard. I was indignant. Why hadn't Mam gone to the rescue?

I was also aware that those neighbours regularly took a razor strop to Cyril, who was about ten years old. The four-inch-wide leather belt was the sort sometimes used today by barbers who anchor the strop to something solid and stroke the razor briskly up and down it until the blade is sharp. Even though Mr Binns's strop wasn't used when Mam and I visited, it looked menacing when I spotted it hanging on the rail under the family's mantelpiece. Mrs Binns would nod meaningfully towards it whenever young Cyril misbehaved.

In the 1930s, most children were spanked, some more severely than others; today this would be considered child abuse. Mam used her hand to slap my legs if I disobeyed; some people, like our neighbours, used a strap. Teachers also caned children if they were unruly, usually the boys. The canes were thin and pliant and even the toughest boys shrieked as they endured what was termed 'six of the best' on their young palms. Most parents approved, asking themselves, how else could their children be taught to behave?

Another little girl, Rita Hurst, lived at Number 9. Her father was a small, rather timid man, and appeared to me quite old. Mrs Hurst, tall, thin, and extremely prim, made even more of a fetish of housework than did my mother. Rita favoured her mother, at least as far as thin and prim went, and she had light brown hair cut in the shingle style of the time and wore unfashionably long dresses. Mam and Mrs Gratrix put this down to the fact that Old Liz—as they privately called Rita's mother—had married and had Rita (young Liz) 'very late'. She had probably been in her late twenties.

On the other side of the canal lived the Preston family. Their daughter, Joy, a small girl with dark brown hair and eyes, was a little older than Margaret; even so we would be invited to her birthday parties. Going to her house was an adventure, since it was some distance from the village and completely surrounded by Chase Woods. It had been a gamekeeper's house in earlier days. One dark, damp evening, we were invited to Joy's birthday party, and Mr Preston, a gnarled, gnome-like man, met us at the bottom of the wood carrying a lantern. The path up to the house was rocky and wet and overhung with oaks and hazelnut trees, all of which made an exciting expedition. The house, too, was lit with lanterns because there was no electricity; it seemed so much more romantic and remote than our own ordinary houses all in a row along the A6.

Because she was older, Margaret went to school a year before I did. This sometimes left me at a loose end, but one day an invitation came for me to go to our milkman Wilmot's farm to play with their little boy, Mickey. Despite the growth of industry, there were still a great number of productive farms throughout the Derwent Valley. Mickey's was one that did not survive as such, but later became a clubhouse for the men who worked at the wireworks; after the wireworks closed, it became a private club.

Going to the farm was an even bigger adventure for me than when I ventured the short distance needed to find flowers for my garden. Mam always took me across the road and watched as I walked to the farm by myself, a distance of about a thousand yards. On one occasion, as I passed the field where Mr Wilmot kept the horse he used for hauling his milk cart, the horse said, 'Good morning, Brenda'. I reported this to Mam on my return home. I firmly believed it, and took no note of Dad's theory that I had been greeted by a neighbour, Mr Waddington, who had been working in his garden nearby.

The gritstone farmhouse had a walled garden, full of flowers and the hum of bees. I particularly remember an old trough Mrs Wilmot had planted with lavender, and the scent when I crushed its leaves with my fingers. Beyond this garden, over a high stone wall, Mrs Wilmot nurtured rows of vegetables and an apple tree. It was sunny and hot in the garden, and as Mickey and I played, I was aware of his mother busy in the kitchen behind us, or coming and going between the house and the dairy. The dairy was cool and smelled delightfully of cream. The farm employed a dairymaid who skimmed cream from the vats to make butter, afterwards sitting for an hour or more laboriously turning the handle of the churn. Beyond the garden wall, as far as the bank of the river, Mr Wilmot's cornfield waved golden in the sun, the poppies among it glowing red. There are few poppies among the wheat today.

Mrs Wilmot, who also worked as the local midwife, was a large, brisk woman; Mam said she was 'educated', and on this occasion it sounded to me as if she approved of our neighbour's learning. Mr Wilmot was small and silent. Every morning he came to our house on Matlock Road with his horse and cart to deliver the day's supply of milk. No one I knew of had a refrigerator, and a daily delivery was necessary. Every morning the farmer would appear at our door, his already bowed shoulders even more bent under the weight of the yoke he carried on which were suspended two buckets containing the milk. This he would ladle into our jug, which Mam afterwards placed on the 'cold slab' in the pantry for safekeeping. To keep flies out of the milk, she covered the mouth of the jug with a small net edged with heavy beads.

One memorable day Mickey took me to one of the barns where, inside the high-ceilinged, whitewashed room, the black-haired, black-bearded farmhand was inexplicably and violently whipping the wheat stalks that littered the floor. Later I learned that he was threshing the wheat, using what even then was an outmoded method. The flailing figure and the whistle of his whip formed a terrifying picture. The man didn't speak or acknowledge us in any way, and eventually Mickey and I crept out of the barn and ran back to the sunny garden.

Farming was still quite primitive on many Derbyshire farms. Although tractors had been invented in the late eighteen hundreds, fields were still often ploughed using horses, the hay 'tedded' and raked with the old machines, the farmer jouncing on the uncomfortable pierced-iron seat behind the horse. Hay was not baled but built into 'cocks' that looked like teepees of loose hay, and were distributed about the field so that they could dry in the sun. Afterwards, the farmer built them into haystacks, chunks of which he would later slice out to use as fodder for his beasts. No farmers I knew made silage.

Living across the road from us in a stone house with a turret and a large garden, was the Kay family. Mr Kay was a manager at the wireworks, and it seemed to Mam that the family had pretensions of grandeur, although she would suspect this of anyone who had what she called a 'pound note' accent. They also employed a gardener and a maid, as did many such families.

The Kays had two children, a boy and a girl, whom they called 'Master Donald' and 'Miss Sarah' when talking about them to us hobbledehoys. Mam, of course, would have no truck with such nonsense and instructed us to call the Kay children by their first names only, although she invariably said Mahster Donald whenever she mentioned the boy to us. She did, however, allow us to go to the Kay's Christmas party, which they held every year for all the children at our end of the village. It was complete with Father Christmas and a present for each of us, so I was always eager to take advantage of the Kay's noblesse oblige. I wonder now if I ought to think more kindly of our old neighbours, but Mam-like I also remember that they expected us to call their son 'Mahster Donald' and their daughter 'Miss Sarah'.

All these children, except for Mickey and the Kay children, would be invited to the tea parties when any one of us living in the row had a birthday. This must have been hard for the children who were excluded, but that possibility didn't occur to me, and I doubt if it occurred to the adults. The reason for the Kay children's exclusion was no doubt because they were several rungs above us in the pecking order; Mickey, despite his mother's profession, was a rung or two below, perhaps because his father's farm was not his own.

When the party was at our house, Mam and Dad carried the table from the back room into the sitting room, after which Mam set the table, arranging a cracker beside each plate. Our first order of business would be to pull the crackers (we hoped with a satis-fying crack) so that we each had a paper hat to wear. Afterwards, Mam brought out tomato sandwiches, followed by jelly, tinned fruit, and the birthday cake, usually Mam's homemade sponge cake, its centre spread with whipped butter, sugar, and a layer of jam. We probably drank weak tea, because I remember the unpleasant feel of Mam's best cups against my lips. These, of a thin, rough material, had been made in Japan, on each a raised pattern of a tree with conical mountains overlooking a river. I hated the feel of those cups but was proud that we were trusted with them at my party.

Before tea, we had games: Pass the Parcel, Musical Chairs, and Oranges and Lemons which was played with two children holding their hands together and high to form an arch, the other children running underneath one by one. The one who was caught when the song came to 'Here comes a candle to light you to bed/Here comes a chopper to chop off your head', was then out of the game. (The game dates from the time of Henry VIII and his unfortunate wife, Anne Boleyn.)

For Musical Chairs we used the gramophone—not one with a huge trumpet, although some of them were probably still in use at the time. Ours had a turntable inside a tall cabinet, the front of which formed the speaker. There was also an arm with replace-able needles, much like the hi-fi sets of the '70s and '80s. Unlike hi-fis, however, this gramophone had to be wound up and the wind kept tight, otherwise, as the mechanism ran down, the sing-ers sounded like drunks reeling out of a pub. The Gratrixes had records, too, and would have lent them, but Mam disapproved of their choices. She was particularly scornful of a recording by Gracie Fields singing, 'The Biggest Aspidistra in the World'. Mrs Gratrix called the singer 'our Gracie'. The singer had a broad Lancashire accent, which Mam said made her 'sound common'. My mother had a broad Derbyshire accent herself, but that didn't seem to earn the epithet.

My parents had about six gramophone records, among them Stanley Holloway's recitations including: 'With 'er 'ead tucked underneath 'er arm, she waaaalks the bloody tower'. Margaret and I loved that one; it was the only time we could say bloody and get away with it. In addition there was a recitation about 'Albert and the Lion', also by Holloway, and twenties songs such as 'When the Red, Red Robin Comes Bob, Bob, Bobbin' Along', 'Abdul the Bulbul Amir', and 'I'm Leanin' on the Lamppost at the Corner of the Street in Case a Certain Little Lady Comes By', sung in a Lancashire accent and with banjo accompaniment by George Formby. Mam had no complaints about his accent, or Stanley Holloway's, although they both came from the Gratrixes' county. These were the songs we used when playing Musical Chairs. Mam was in charge of the gramophone; I was not allowed to touch it until much later.

Perhaps there were presents, but I don't remember receiving any at the birthday parties. I do remember a black baby doll I received from my parents for my seventh birthday and carrying her out into the garden. Again, it was a hot, sunny morning; there was musk in the flower borders, and a few of the American pillar roses that wound over an archway into the vegetable garden were already in bloom. The doll had been dressed for me by Grandmother Wallis in a little knitted frock and bonnet in orange wool. She was a much-loved toy, called, I'm sorry to say, my Sambo doll. She lost her pottery face a couple of times owing to my clumsiness, and Margaret's father took her to what I was told was the doll's hospital in Derby.

Of all the friends I made as a small child on Matlock Road, I remained in touch only with Margaret. She died in January 2013.

CHAPTER 8
The Cromford Canal

Gregory Tunnel

Leawood Pump House

UP THE LANE CLOSE to our house lay the Cromford Canal. One day Dad got it into his head that we should use the nettles growing beside the canal path as a vegetable, his argument being that nettles were full of iron and would be good for us. After all, he pointed out, we saved a lot of money by gathering the pounds of bilberries and blackberries that became available each summer on the surrounding moors and making them into jam, so why not gather this free green vegetable? Although my father was now doing well at his work, perhaps because of the struggle he'd had earlier in the Depression, it seemed sensible to him to take advantage of this free food. Mam was certain it was a terrible idea and told him that if he brought nettles into the house, he could cook them himself. Peter was walking by this time, and Dad took us both, along with his big-gauntleted driving gloves, a paper bag, and a pair of scissors, on a nettle expedition. We went along the canal towpath as far as Chase Bridge, Dad clipping nettles as we went. When we took them home, Mam said, probably correctly, 'They'll have been peed on by dogs,' and as she had threatened, she refused to have anything to do with them. Dad put them into a saucepan, covered them with water, and cooked them on the trivet over the fire. I expect he ate them, no doubt defiantly, but I refused to—nettles sting, don't they? I don't think he repeated that experiment.

In my youth, some of the locals called the Cromford Canal 't'cut', presumably because it had literally been hacked out of the landscape. The waterway, which is over fourteen miles long, twenty-five feet wide, and quite shallow, was connected to another canal, the Erewash, which took goods on flat-bottomed barges as far as Nottingham. William Jessup and Benjamin Outram, partners in the Butterly Company, had the canal built in 1794, using the skills of Dutch labourers imported for the task. A now-defunct pub at Crich was named 'The Jovial Dutchman' in honour of these men. At its peak of activity, the barges carried not only spun cotton from Arkwright's mills at Cromford but coal from Ripley and limestone from Crich, as well as coke, iron ore, gritstone, and lead, all either taken aboard or delivered at wharfs up and down the waterway. The barges were narrow so that they could usually pass each other, and there was also an occasional 'passing place', such as one finds today along one-lane roads. At one time, notices at the ends of the tunnels told the 'up' and 'down' bargees the hours in which they were allowed to negotiate a tunnel that was too narrow for two barges to pass.

As a child, as I fished for tadpoles, I watched the barges languidly making their way along the canal, each barge about twenty feet long and quite narrow, with a small cabin at the back for the bargee and sometimes his family. Each barge was hauled along the canal by a horse that walked along the towpath. When the vessel came to a bridge or the occasional tunnel, the horse, which was too large to continue along the path under the bridge, was unharnessed and led by the bargee's wife—or a boy hired for the task—up a path over the side of the bridge and down again to the towpath on the other side to rejoin the barge. Meanwhile, the bargee propelled his craft under the bridge or tunnel by pushing with his hands or, lying on his back, with his feet against the roof. Bargees were colourful and friendly folk who would wave to us children who stared shyly at them from the towpath. Dad knew several of these men, and it was a big adventure for me when one of them invited us to come aboard for a ride. In the 1840s, before the road was extended along the valley to Matlock Bath, railway passengers wishing to visit that town sometimes disembarked at Ambergate, took a canal boat as far as Cromford, and then walked the rest of the way.

Cromford Canal (John Grain)

Our family spent a great deal of time along the canal towpath, which, with fields and woods on either side, made for a pleasant walk. The woods were of elm, alder, rowan, and hawthorn and were filled with bluebells for us to pick in the spring. The nearby fields, full of grazing cattle, were golden with buttercups in spring and summer. Today, the canal is still there, apart from a small length beyond what were the limekilns at Ambergate. The towpath between Whatstandwell and Ambergate is now a nature reserve, the rest is weeded and mown by the County Council, and the water is periodically freed of its burden of duckweed and reeds. There is a small museum at High Peak, plus another museum, gift shop, and café in what were Arkwright's mills at the north end of the canal at Cromford. T'cut has lost its original usefulness, and in 1944 was closed as a waterway. Nowadays it is the pleasurable haunt of hikers and birders.

CHAPTER 9

How We Celebrated

Christmas in Derbyshire (John Grain)

'BREN, HE'S BEEN!' PETE whispered excitedly.

It was Christmas morning, still dark and our parents fast asleep. We surreptitiously crept to the ends of our beds to feel our parcels and try to guess what was in them. At this early stage, we didn't put the light on for fear Dad would yell at us to put it off again.

After examination of the parcels came the actual unpacking, still in the dark, of the stockings. These usually contained old favourites: a few crayons, some chocolate pennies, a sugar mouse, and a tangerine. Tangerines seemed exotic to us because they came from Spain, only at Christmas, wrapped in silver paper and delivered in a wooden crate. These were traditional, and we were disappointed if any of our favourites failed to appear. We then ate the tangerine and the pennies, and, as light began at last to seep round the edges of the curtains, we opened our presents.

Unlike today's children, we were not inundated with so many toys that we didn't know what to play with first. There would be a present from our parents—in the early years, a new doll or doll's pram for me, a wooden train for Pete. Later, we received second- or third-hand tricycles, and later still, two-wheelers. The year I began Bailey's Grammar School, Dad gave me a small desk. My Wallis grandparents and Aunt Flo always gave me books. Granny Durward was too poor, but Aunt Gladys, knowing my love of reading, also gave me a book, usually a so-called *Bumper Book for Girls*, or some other large tome that contained stories, poems, and riddles. Our parents also gave us games over the years: Tiddlywinks, Ludo, Snakes and Ladders, picture puzzles, and the like. As time went on and the war began, presents became fewer. By then, Pete and I knew the truth about Father Christmas, and it was sister Beryl, and later brother Gib who was born during the war, who received the few games and toys that were available. At this time, my mother gave me chocolates—before they disappeared because of the war. Dad gave me money, and once produced for me a pendant with a background of diamante and a single artificial pearl.

We always had a tree, as did most country families, even the poorest ones whose children went into the woods to saw off a small branch from a conifer; others took home sprigs of holly. Dad usually brought home a tree he bought at a market somewhere on his travels, leaving Mam to set it up. At Ambergate, its post was on top of the gramophone cabinet in the front room. We had some few baubles to put on it, including glass balls, icicles, and little clip-on candleholders with real wax candles in them about the size of those now used for birthday cakes. This was instead of electric 'fairy lights'. The candles were highly dangerous and could be lit for only a short time while we stood beneath the twinkling tree, holding our breaths with delight.

Margaret and I spent a lot of time and glue before Christmas fastening strips of coloured paper into circles and afterwards stringing them together to make the garlands that we looped about our respective sitting rooms; I used mine to decorate the fireplace mirror and strung them from one picture rail to another. 'Like a blessed jungle,' Dad would complain.

Easter was largely a church or chapel celebration in the 1930s. These concerned Margaret and Rita, who attended the services with their families; we secular Wallises had only Easter eggs, Tom Moreten being the donor after he and Aunt Gladys began 'going together'. Tom's Easter gifts were always huge, elaborate affairs consisting of a chocolate egg for each of us, with sugar chickens or little flowers around it for decoration. Uncle Tom was a great favourite at 5, Matlock Road.

Mother's Day didn't exist as such in the 1930s but was Hallmark-produced many years later. Instead, the churches held what was called Mothering Sunday in May, when there was a special service at the church or chapel, after which the children ran to the fields where they gathered bouquets of wild flowers to present to their mothers. Again, we were not included.

Every year, Ambergate held a carnival on what we called the Rec (the recreation ground off the A6 opposite Wibberly's shop) that was organized by a special committee. There were the usual booths with baked goods made by Women's Institute members, coconut shies, a merry-go-round, and, some years, donkey rides. Often we were entertained by the tooting of a brass band from some other village that marched ahead of the one or two floats assembled near Wilmot's farm before progressing to the Recreation Ground. The floats consisted of Wilmot's old farm wagons, in which groups of children rode in fancy dress pretending they were Queen Boadicea and her court, or Robin Hood and his Merry Men, or a fairy queen and her entourage. The Rec was almost a mile from our house at the other end of the village, and Mam walked us there, Pete in his pushchair wearing one of his little 'buster suits' and a white sunhat, me clinging to the handle.

One year, the carnival included a gymkhana—show jumping—in which horsemen and women competed for prizes. This was held in one of Wilmot's fields between the farmhouse and the River Derwent, and for me the big excitement of the day was when a horsewoman fell from her horse at a jump and had to be carried off the field on an improvised stretcher—a farm gate. The day was hot and sunny, and the organizers held a fancy dress parade for the children; Mam dressed me as Little Red Riding Hood for the day.

Another kind of 'amusement' was when Margaret and I were seven and six years old, and our mothers took us to Matlock to attend a children's fancy dress ball. The dance was held in the Town Hall opposite the police station at the bottom of Bank Road. Margaret and I had been dressed up in paper costumes provided by our mothers, Margaret as a tulip, I as a daffodil, and for a dreadful hour or so, we 'danced', pushing and pulling one another round the dance floor and falling over each other's feet. I assume our mothers thought we'd find it fun. Then came the judging, when we children were lined up in several rows, Margaret and I to the rear, to be minutely inspected. Some dreadful girls (I looked on them with scorn) stood on tippy-toe and held out the hems of their dresses. Naturally, one of these was chosen to be Queen of the Dance. Grouchy and fed up, we glowered until at last we were taken home.

At the other end of the holiday spectrum (the Protestant end, that is), we celebrated Guy Fawkes Day. Unlike other festivals, such as Halloween, the Fifth of November is not for export, especially not to countries where there is a large Catholic population. This holiday commemorates the day in 1605 when Catholic Guy Fawkes and fellow conspirators hid twenty barrels of gunpowder in the cellars of Westminster in a plot to blow up both King James the First and Parliament in retaliation for the suppression of

Catholicism. The actual instigator of the plot was Robert Catesby, but Guy had been recruited to do the dirty deed because he was a soldier, had been in Spain for some years, and was not so well known to the authorities. Guy and his helpers were apprehended before the gunpowder went off; he was tortured until he revealed the names of his co-conspirators before being executed in front of the Parliament building. Catesby was killed by government troops when resisting capture.

I doubt if any of us thought about the anti-Catholic history of Guy Fawkes Day, even when we were in the process of fashioning a 'Guy' to be incinerated on our bonfires. It may be that Catholic children were not allowed by their parents to participate in Guy Fawkes Day, but I certainly don't remember hearing that this ever happened. However, there were no Catholic children at the Ambergate or Fritchley schools since we were all either chapel or Church of England, and I knew of only one Catholic at my grammar school. At morning assembly, after the Headmaster had made his announcements and before we launched into morning prayers, one little girl solemnly left the hall, and we waited politely until she was gone before proceeding. I don't remember anyone teasing the girl about her religion, and I like to think she enjoyed Guy Fawkes Day as much as the rest of us.

Just before Bonfire Night, small boys hauled their Guys about the village, pleading 'Penny for the Guy', money they used to buy the fireworks, which added to the joy of the celebration. Children also wandered the streets or countryside collecting burnable material from which to make their bonfire. In towns they gathered wooden crates from the markets; in the country we scavenged twigs from the local woods. At Ambergate, Dad set up our bonfire at the end of the garden, a modest affair of sticks, newspapers, and a log or two, and held his lighter to it just after sunset, signalling the start of festivities, when we children, Pete and I, began to dance round the bonfire waving our sparklers. After that, Dad activated the jumping jacks—little packets of gunpowder that exploded in sequence and leaped among our feet, making us jump too. He launched rockets from the necks of beer bottles and pinned the Catherine wheels (named for the martyred St Catherine) to the rose trellis. When he lit them, we retired immediately—as the slips of paper attached to the fireworks admonished us— to watch the whirling sparks from a safe distance. Mam always made a special 'bonfire toffee' for the occasion out of treacle and a smattering of nuts, cooked on a tray in the oven until it looked like black glass. Margaret, Rita, and other children from along the row often dropped in from their toffee-less bonfires. During the war there were no Guy Fawkes celebrations; a country dotted with fires would have been too great a boon to the Luftwaffe.

Halloween customs had pretty much died out when I was a child. Centuries before it had been the night the ghosts walked. There were no Halloween lanterns connected with it and no celebration that I remember; it is only since the war that jack-o'-lanterns appear to have swum the Atlantic, making Halloween once again a celebration in Britain.

In November a more sober ceremony took place on the eleventh day of the eleventh month at the eleventh hour, the day and time the Armistice was signed that ended the First World War. At school the teachers regaled us with patriotic stories, and at eleven o'clock we stood, heads bowed, and kept two minutes silence in honour of those who had died at Remy Wood or Ypres. Outside on the streets, when a nearby church clock chimed the hour, passers-by paused and men removed their hats. What we then called the Great War was barely fifteen years behind us; it would shadow our lives and particularly those of our parents for many years.

CHAPTER 10

I Find God

The Cross at Crich

RELIGION WAS NEVER MENTIONED at 5, Matlock Road; no 'Gentle Jesus, meek and mild' for us. I suspect that, for Mam, it was again a matter of class. People who attended church were 'them snobs', along with ''ypocrits' and other such fauna. Dad never said anything about religion at all, and Granny Wallis once told me that Granddad was agnostic. If so, he was a typical product of Victorian scepticism that began after Darwin and Wallace's origin of species hypotheses. Granny and Flo went to church now and then—mainly at Easter and Christmas—but again, never got round to telling me what their beliefs were, if any. At 2, St John's Terrace, it was a subject that never arose.

Nevertheless, religion had a much larger following then than now, when most churches have minute congregations. Among my friends, Margaret and Rita went to Sunday school at the Ambergate C of E church, as did most of the children who lived along Matlock Road. I have a vivid memory of Margaret in one of the knee-length dresses and straw cloche hats of the period, running up the steps of the church. (Why do these vignettes stick in the memory? There was nothing traumatic about the scene as far as I know, except that I was not running up the steps, too.) Margaret and Rita never saw fit to tell me what went on at Sunday school, and I never saw fit to ask. It was enough for me that Mam didn't want me messing with snobs and hypocrites.

Largely because of my lack of religious instruction, it came as a shock when I began school at the age of five and the first thing the other children did in the morning was bow their heads and follow our teacher in the 'Ah Fah.' 'Ah Fah,' they intoned, 'chart n'evven.' It was a complete mystery to me, another of those odd things that arose when I was away from the safety of Mam. But I was a conforming child, so I bowed my head too, moved my lips, and murmured something, peering to left and right at my classmates from under my brows. It took several weeks for me to fathom what the words were, not that they made a great deal of sense to me when they were fathomed.

It was not long, though, before the teacher, Miss Beecham, enlightened me. She was a farmer's daughter, large and red-cheeked, and began each day with a prayer and Bible stories. No laws existed about separating church and state as in other countries; the King was head of the Church of England, and that was that. Miss Beecham taught us tales from both the Old and the New Testaments: Daniel in the lion's den, Joseph and his coat of many colours, Cain and Abel, plus a great many stories of the Gentle Jesus, meek and mild variety. I was entranced. It seemed, if I understood Miss Beecham aright, that I could say some words 'to the close and holy dark' and someone would take care of me, just in the way Mam did, only with even more authority. I was all for that.

However, I was savvy enough not to tell Mam about my instant conversion, and I don't think she was ever aware of my fervent prayers after she had tucked me up in my bed in the little box room and had closed the door. I prayed for everyone, constantly; it was my way of keeping them safe in a dangerous world. And somehow, to me, it was beginning to seem a dangerous world. I came to the conclusion many years later that Mam, too, had been afraid of the world, and this had conveyed itself to me. In fact, my mother's most constant phrase was 'I'm afraid' or, more often, 'I'm frightened'. Also, there were already sinister stirrings in Germany and the Far East that were beginning to alarm the grownups, and I gradually picked up their unease.

A little later, when I was six or so, I became aware of death after our small black-and-white dog, Peter, was run over on the road outside our front gate. (Odd, yes; my parents had named their dog Peter before brother Pete came along. I can only assume that they really liked the name.) In any case, I suddenly knew that my beloved Mam and Dad would die one day, and I would, too. That was real terror, and from then on I sent prayers feverishly into the ceiling of my little room, night after night, to the effect that if we had to die, then God should let all of us—Mam, Dad, me, even brother Pete—die at exactly the same moment. It also occurred to me that maybe God would like a little gift. I'm not sure of my motives: was it that if I gave Him a gift, maybe He would forgive me a transgression or two? Or was I testing Him out, trying to prove to myself that He really was there and could do miracles, such as coming down, taking whatever gift I offered? At this distance I think the motivation was a mix of awe and self-service, although I can't be certain of that. In any case I looked among my toys for something special and decided that a doll's bonnet filled with some of my beads would be just the thing to give to the Lord. These I stashed behind the copper hot water tank in the bathroom. I believe I even put a note in it, although I probably couldn't write very well at the time.

Apparently the age of miracles was not yet past, because the bonnet and beads disappeared! I'll never forget the mixture of joy and fear I felt when I looked behind that water tank and found… nothing at all. Mam hadn't taken it, I was sure of that; if she had, she would have asked what the dickens my doll's bonnet was doing behind the tank. Moreover, the bonnet would have surfaced again on my doll's head. It never did, and I was left totally hooked.

CHAPTER 11

The Games We Played

NOW AND AGAIN, IN summer, the River Derwent was at a low enough ebb so that a sandbank was exposed just below the Ha'penny Bridge near Woodbine Cottage (now named Trilithon Lodge). On warm days, my mother, Mrs Hurst, and Mrs Gratrix would take us children down to the river 'for a paddle'. None of us could swim, including the mothers, so we had to keep close to the sand spit. Just a little way out, the river ran fast, and a local swimmer had drowned there, so we children were on a very tight rein.

Nevertheless, it was a thrill to be able to paddle in water so close to home as if it were the seaside.

Winter games, at Ambergate, Fritchley, and later at Ernest Bailey's School, always involved a slide. At the first sign of snow, and even frost, we would make a slide in the schoolyard and burnish it up by in turn running and then taking off down it, arms flailing. Little boys in their slippery segged boots were particularly good at this.

Solitary games, after nursery years, were usually ball games in which I tossed the ball under a raised leg, or over my head, or round my back, caught it, and tossed it again. There were rules and points attached to the game that I no longer remember. On desperate days, I would be reduced to blowing bubbles through a small clay pipe, using a pan of soapsuds provided by Mam.

About this time, I began to collect cigarette cards from Dad's Players cigarettes, or the cheaper Woodbines my uncles favoured. Sometimes the cards depicted football players, or field flowers, or trees, but the ones I preferred were of British kings and queens. I had a book to stick them into as I collected them, each with a picture of the monarch and some text that told something about his or her reign. Woodbine packets had another meaning for us children. We believed that when we saw a 'Willie Woodbine' packet discarded on the ground, we had only to put our foot on it, say some magic words, and we would find a sixpence. No one ever did.

I had a second-hand, three-wheeled bike at this time that was later exchanged for a two-wheeler. Jack and Uncle Bud taught me to ride the two-wheeler in the alley behind Granny Durward's house in Matlock. One or the other of the uncles ran along behind me holding the bicycle seat, and when he felt I could ride on my own, he let go of it, leaving me to wobble, usually into the nearby wall. After a series of barked—that is, scraped—knuckles I finally got the hang of it. (No training wheels back then.)

Of course we also had the nameless games children played which the adults called 'messing about'. One such involved Margaret and me illegally 'going on the bank,' that is, the railway bank behind our houses, a steep, grassy rise with lots of dog daisies in season, a bunch of which could be used to sweeten up our mothers if we were caught. We were not supposed to play on the railway bank because the adults were afraid we would end up playing on the rails. We were too savvy for that, because a man had been killed at the level crossing at Wingfield station one foggy November evening, and that was enough for us.

Margaret and I also made excursions into the fields that surrounded the Top Hag above the limekilns (later a collection point for North Sea gas). There we made bouquets of cowslips and lady smocks to bring home, or fish for tadpoles in the canal. On one occasion, in a highly dangerous manoeuvre, Margaret crawled over the canal by way of a bridge that carried a large water pipe. My friend made a successful crossing while I stayed prudently on the bank and waited for her to fall in.

Our parents seemed to have no fear about us roaming the fields and woods, and, indeed, I remember no occasion throughout my childhood, including the war years when soldiers and Italian prisoners of war were about, during which any child was molested. I don't think it was only luck. I'm sure children were abused in some places, but the crime didn't seem as widespread as it is today. Of course, incidents could have been under-reported, although I have a feeling that crimes of violence were fewer then; they certainly were in our part of Derbyshire. The single murder I remember from my childhood shocked everyone. Today, in London or Edinburgh, in Chicago or Los Angeles, they are a nightly item on the evening news.

For other entertainment, we sometimes listened to the wireless. This was an old Pye radio about a foot tall with a curved top; its front, the speaker, was made of some sort of fabric behind a fancy wooden grille. I listened, not very often, to Children's Hour, which was broadcast at five each afternoon when 'Uncle Mac' read a story in his posh, BBC accent. Later, with more enthusiasm, I became an Ovalteenie, sending in the coupons I found in tins of Ovaltine, receiving in return a round, brass badge that looked rather like an old penny. I wore it proudly on my lapel to indicate my new, lofty status. The Ovalteenie song, which aired, I assume, on Radio Luxembourg because the BBC was without advertising, is with me yet:

We are the Ovalteenies,
Little girls and boys.
Make your request,
We'll not refuse you,
We are here just to amuse you.
Would you like a song or story?
Would you share our joys?

At games and sports we're more than keen,
No merrier children could be seen,
Because we all drink Ovaltine,
We're happy girls and boys.

I even remember the tune.

On our Pye radio, we also learned about Post Toasties and Force, early kinds of corn flake, the latter advertised by a sort of 'Eat Your Wheaties' ditty:

High o'er the fence,
O'er the fence leaps Sunny Ji...him.
Force is the food,
Is the food that raises hi...him.

About this time, Margaret and I were both given a gift subscription to the first Mickey Mouse comic produced in Britain and were soon enthralled by the adventures of 'Unca' Mickey and his two nephews, Minnie of the enormous shoes, and Goofy and Donald Duck. If I had saved those first issues, I'd now be rich! Later, Peter was given the Beano comic, which I believe is still produced.

The cinema, or 'the pictures', as we called it, was a rare treat for Margaret, and aside from my occasional trips to the Hay Barn, for me also. On one occasion Mrs Gratrix and Mam took us to Belper to see a film starring Shirley Temple, and although our two mothers appeared to enjoy themselves, I sat glowering throughout. The film was sentimental in the extreme, but I doubt that I was a sophisticated critic at five or six. I have continued to scorn simpering women and sentimentality ever since, but on that occasion I was no doubt jealous of Shirley's curls. I also disliked the occasion because a ragged man outside the cinema asked Mam and Mrs Gratrix for money. I thought he looked hungry, and I was saddened when they refused. Seeing my distress, Mam assured me that the man would have only spent the money on beer, an excuse that today would have also included drugs.

Games in the 1930s tended to be seasonal. Now, outdoor games of any sort have been pretty much overridden by the X-Box, the Wii, and other such pursuits, but when I was a child, in the spring just before Easter we brought out our shuttlecocks and battledores—a racquet and badminton bird—and tried to hit the bird into the air as many times as possible without letting it touch the ground, thus deciding the number of pancakes to eat on Shrove Tuesday, Pancake Day. Mam always made pancakes then, although I don't remember eating more than two, each as big as a dinner plate and deliciously thin, sprinkled with sugar plus a squeeze of lemon or orange juice.

The game of hoops appeared after Easter. Margaret and I each had a large metal hoop, similar in size to the hula-hoops that came later, which we propelled along with a metal stick attached to the hoop. We would race up and down our entryway, holding our sticks to the rim of the hoop, pushing it forward and trying to see who could keep it upright and rolling the longest.

We played hopscotch and marbles in the schoolyard, along with games of tag. Our hopscotch grid was pretty much as it is today: a square drawn with chalk on the school yard, followed by two squares side by side, then another single, and so on, ending with double squares. The skipping child tossed a small, flat stone onto the first square and then proceeded down the grid, first hopping to the next square or squares, picking up the stone while standing on one foot and tossing her stone onto the next square. The idea was to avoid stepping on, or tossing a stone onto, one of the lines. We also had a grid that I have not seen lately, consisting of squares drawn to make a spiral, each square becoming smaller and smaller until the grid ended with one square in the middle.

Also in the schoolyard skipping ropes put in an appearance. Two girls took the ends of the rope (usually a piece of clothesline provided by a mother) and turned it while a long line of girls ran in, skipped once, and skipped out again. (Boys scorned this game.) Sometimes the turners had two ropes, one in each hand, and turned the ropes towards the middle, one after the other, forcing us to skip twice as fast as with a single rope. There were rhymes attached to skipping, such as 'salt, mustard, vinegar, pepper', as the ropes were turned faster and faster.

Whips and tops were another springtime favourite. In this, I wound my whip tightly around the stem of a mushroom-shaped top and flung it out onto the schoolyard, where the action of the whip as it unwound caused it to spin. I kept the spin going by continually whipping the top. This game brought out the artist in even the dullest girl, and we would use coloured chalks to make spirals or diamonds on the heads of our tops so that the pattern would whirl like a kaleidoscope as they spun.

CHAPTER 12

Going on Our Holidays

Brenda on a Scottish moor

BEFORE THE WAR, EVEN during the Depression, Dad's job was secure enough for us to take brief holidays. The same was true of many of my friends' families, because with the advent of paid holidays for factory and other workers, the founding in 1930 of the Youth Hostel Association, and later the development of Butlin's cheap holiday camps at Skegness, a holiday away from home became possible for the first time for many of the working class.

For us, this meant spending a week at the seaside. On one trip we went by car to Looe in Cornwall with its steep little streets and the bay with its glorious wide sands. On these seaside trips, we stayed in boarding houses where, if the landlady was a dragon, we had to spend the bulk of the day outside, rain or shine. Fortunately, at Looe the proprietor provided a sitting room where we could go in wet weather to play with the few board games she had provided.

Other years we went to Skegness on the east coast. 'Skegness is So Bracing!' declared the slogan below a picture of a rubicund sailor in knee-high boots, gripping his pipe between his teeth and leaping (bracedly?) along a beach. These advertisements appeared on huge sheets of tin attached to the walls of every railway station platform. (Another such sign said enigmatically, 'Hovis'. I was greatly intrigued by this, until I discovered that Hovis was some kind of bread.) On the east coast, the tide goes out so far that at low tide it is almost impossible to know where the sea begins, which made the beach ideal for the exciting sand yachts with sails and wheels that skimmed over the wide sands. There was usually enough wind for them to get up a quite lively speed.

Rhyll, in Wales, was another holiday destination, where I was once thrilled to see a woman wearing the black cloak and tall, witch-like hat of the Welsh national costume. At every seaside place, there was a paddling pool for children, often with quite elaborate grottos. Of course we took the usual buckets and spades for the sand, and there were donkey rides, our mounts so wide that our legs stuck out almost at right angles. It was always cold on the beaches, even when the sun shone, and the sand rasped against my legs when Mam dried me off after I'd 'had a paddle'.

Arrival at our boarding house was always a fraught moment. One year in Scarborough, Mam absolutely refused to enter the accommodation Dad had reserved by post. 'A filthy hole', she declared with a toss of her head (I'm not sure how she knew). We drove past without stopping and went to find a room in a hotel. A costly holiday, no doubt.

If the digs appeared acceptable, there was the unpacking to be done, the beds minutely inspected (Mam), the proximity of a pub looked into (Dad), and our nearness to the shore paced out (Pete and I). After that, the holiday had truly begun. For us children it was all breathlessly exciting, and we spent hours making sand castles, collecting shells and seaweed, paddling in the pools along the shore, jumping over the waves, and taking rides on the little donkeys that jingled up and down the beach. A week seemed endless. To wear for 'swimming', Mam bought us costumes made of some sort of artificial fabric that clung to us embarrassingly when wet. For paddling, little girls, and even grown women, tucked their skirts into the elasticized legs of their bloomers; men rolled up their trousers, and to keep the sun off, tied knots in the corners of large white handkerchiefs to wear as caps. Sartorially elegant we were not.

The big treat for me, however, was an excursion I always took with Dad. On at least one afternoon during the holiday, as Mam put Peter to bed for his nap, Dad and I walked down to the end of the pier for the concert party given by a group called The Pierrots. This consisted of singing by a 'soubrette' rather past her prime, but always 'fresh from her triumph in the West End'; jugglers and magicians and men sawing women in half; acrobats, clowns, and two men in bowler hats and loud suits making what I suspect now were extremely dirty jokes. Everyone laughed uproariously, including me.

All this was glorious for children, but Mam hated it. 'I hate holidays!' she would exclaim as Peter and I got together our buckets and spades or went off to boast to the neighbour children that we were 'going on our holidays'. I expect it was a great headache for my mother because she had all the preparations to make, the washing beforehand and afterwards, packing, the sandwiches for the journey, keeping two overexcited children under control. Dad gave her no help whatever with all this—it was woman's work, a rule that my mother herself accepted. Peter and I kept our heads down until we were on the road; after that, it was Dad's turn.

My father was a very nervous man and driving us to the seaside made him tense and irritable, which was not helped by the fact that Peter was usually on Mam's knee in the front seat, puking his heart out. Pete was a bad traveller; fortunately, I was not. The car was overladen with all the things Mam thought we might need: clothes for wet weather, and for dry; clothes for hot weather, and for cold; as well as all the buckets, spades, and other paraphernalia Pete and I wanted to take along. Aunt Gladys was often with us, crammed beside me in the back seat.

Our Jowett was not robust, and it had a high, partly cloth roof, running boards, and celluloid windows that gave a yellowish tinge to the countryside. Later, we had an Austin 7, which was more up-to-date, but considerably smaller than the Jowett. In either car, to turn right Dad had to wind down the window and put his arm straight out, no matter if there was rain, sleet, or snow. I don't remember the signal for a left turn, but it might have been the one I learned many years later in Washington for a right turn: an arm out of the window, elbow bent. Later, cars had red 'flickers': little, red oblong lights with a pointed end that 'flicked' out of the side of the car above the front doors, one on the left side and one on the right. Later, of course, came the 'winkers' we know today.

On one seaside journey before the war, we all gasped as we looked up into the sky where a biplane soared. 'They can go more than one hundred miles an hour!' Dad informed us. We could hardly believe such speed, or the fact that we had actually spotted an aeroplane. The almost constant roar of jets and the sight of their contrails were long in the future.

Another memory, this time of a holiday at Rhyll, involves Dad's and my narrow escape from drowning. At low tide, we had wandered a long way out towards where the Irish Sea was only a thin ribbon on the horizon. What we hadn't noticed was that the tide was coming in unevenly and that two great arms of it were about to join and cut us off. Neither of us could swim. As it was, Dad had to roll up his trousers and piggyback me through an area of deep, black mud in order to get us to the esplanade before the sea overwhelmed us.

'Don't tell Mammy,' he warned me, as he scraped mud from his turn-ups. I don't think I told her, although our escape had been a near thing.

Uncle Gib and Dad

For all of us, even for Mam, Scottish holidays were the best. North of the Border Dad went out shooting rabbits with Uncle Gib, or fishing in the various lochs; Mam and Auntie Rose, Grandmother Wallis's sister, hit it off and happily nattered together over the chores. For all of us, being in Scotland was better than all the Pierrots in Wales standing on the wall in a row. I loved Scotland and all things Scottish: cairns, heather, bog myrtle, hills, and, at the romantic age of eleven, my father's very handsome Scottish cousin.

One of the earliest Scottish holidays of all was a trip Dad, Auntie Flo, and I took just after Peter was born, when I was about four. No wonder my mother took a dim view of her in-laws when, having given birth, she was now confined to bed for the next ten days while her family and Flo went gallivanting. Possibly it was a help to have me out of the way for a while, but I could have stayed at The Beeches or with my Matlock grandmother, and then Dad would have been available to give at least moral support.

The three of us stayed with a Mrs Agnew at Cairn Ryan on the Wigtonshire coast. I remember little about it, except that Mr Agnew was a fisherman and his wife used some of his glass floats as decoration on either side of the front door. I also got into trouble with Dad by refusing to eat a trout he had caught. There is a snap, taken that same day on the shore of the loch at nearby Castle Kennedy, showing me glowering under my fringe. There is a family story about Mrs Agnew (whom we visited with my mother on subsequent occasions) trying to 'pod', as if they were peas, some runner beans we had brought her from our garden. In those days our Scots relatives ate very little green stuff, in fact, until some years after the war, the only vegetables they ate with their excellent beef were turnips (neeps), potatoes (taties), cabbage, and leeks. We seldom saw oranges or bananas for sale in Newton-Stewart shops in the 1930s.

Aunt Rose and Uncle Gib

The best of the Scottish holidays were spent with Aunt Rose and Uncle Gib at Polbae in Scotland. Uncle Gib was a big Scotsman whose mother, he told us, 'had the garlic'; that is, spoke Gaelic. While staying at Polbae, we made excursions to various seaside towns in the area: Wigton, Girvan, Stranraer, and Ballantrae in its little cove with its small, walled harbour. We all loved Ballantrae, which is why our parents used that name for the house they built at Fritchley; later still, it was the name my husband Joe and I gave to our house in Beverly Shores, Indiana.

Polbae was in the moors about ten miles from Newton-Stewart, Wigtonshire, on what was the estate of a Major Fox. He had been Uncle Gib's officer during the Great War, and afterwards had offered him a job as gamekeeper. The Big House is a ruin now, although the cottages are still inhabited, but for me the regiments of pines planted since by the Forestry Preserve have swallowed up the once-magnificent moorland vistas. I suppose I should approve of these regimental rows of conifers because they are attempts to reintroduce the carbon-devouring trees that covered the area before man came along with his sheep. Unfortunately, the trees make me feel, to use a Derbyshire word, 'mithered', meaning bothered or smothered.

Even in her late forties, Auntie Rose was a stout, grey-haired lady; I loved her with a passion. She and Uncle Gib were assigned two adjoining keeper's cottages at Polbae, one they used as the dwelling, the other as an annex with storage space and a room where they kept the large tin bath. The lavatory was in a small hut in the wood behind the house. When we visited, the Dewar children, Annie, Peter, Bertie (Gilbert), and Rosie, slept in the 'other house', while we four crowded into the main cottage with Uncle Gib and Aunt Rose.

Better than the seaside, at least for me, were the moors surrounding Polbae; they smelled intoxicatingly of bog myrtle,
peat, bracken, and heather. When we were very young, we were
not allowed to wander far on the moor, although I went with
Dad and Uncle Gib when they were shooting rabbits and was
given the dead rabbits to hold. I hated that and tried vainly to
wipe the blood from their eyes. Uncle Gib often took me with
him when he was setting snares: wire nooses attached to sticks,
which he drove into the ground and disguised with bits of
bracken and grass. I was always sorry if we caught anything, but
none of this stopped me from eating Aunt Rose's rabbit stew
with gusto. On later holidays, after I was twelve or so, I was
allowed to roam the moors all day like a gypsy, and shepherds
on nearby estates kept Uncle Gib informed of my whereabouts.
(He worried that I would get mired in one of the many bogs that
littered the moor.) 'The lassie's way over to Loch Maberry', they
told him, or 'The Knowe', or 'Tannie Laggie'.

When I was nine, I took another holiday with Mrs Gratrix
and Margaret to Manchester, where we visited Margaret's grandparents. During this excursion, we visited Blackpool Tower, (supposedly like the Eiffel Tower, though shorter), where we heard
Reginald Dixon playing popular ditties on an organ that rose
majestically out of the floor. We had heard Dixon on our Pye
wireless at home, so this for us was a media event. We also took
a tram down the Blackpool promenade to admire the illumina-
tions: coloured fairy lights attached to various structures along
the way, including the pier, bus shelters, and the fence between

the promenade and the beach. The lights helped form scenes from nursery rhymes and children's stories, and would probably seem very tame to today's children, but in the thirties when we were six or seven, it was a wonderland.

The Cottages, Polbae

CHAPTER 13

In Good Health and Bad

MAM OFTEN USED HER own nostrums on us, including an iodine locket, which she bought from a gypsy woman who came to the door. It was supposed to protect me against 'Derbyshire neck', the local name for goitre, caused by a lack of iodine in Derbyshire soils. (I've heard it called Pennsylvania neck in Pennsylvania.) Grandmother Wallis had a goitre—a large, swollen mass on one side of her neck, and Mam was determined I shouldn't 'go the same way'.

As a child I was often ill, as was Peter. In Ambergate the narrow valleys of the Derwent and Amber Rivers trapped the autumn mists and this, augmented by exhaust from vehicles on the A6 road, gave us frequent fogs. Our houses too, all of them heated by coal fires, added to the unhealthy air, while the trains puffed out their own rain of soot and smoke. Sometimes in winter, the fog was so thick that it came curling into the rooms at No. 5 and hung about the corners of our ceilings in yellow tendrils.

Mam's other curatives, in addition to the camphorated oil chest rubs, included Friar's Balsam, a brown substance that she put into boiling water in a basin, afterwards ordering me to bend my head over the steam, drape it with a towel, and 'stay there and breathe' until the water had cooled. This was supposed to 'loosen the phlegm'.

Most mothers of the time tormented their children by mandating various elixirs to be taken, one spoonful at a time, after breakfast. Each day I would have to swallow something called Scott's Emulsion, which was probably some sort of fish oil, followed by a mixture called Brimstone and Treacle. The label claimed that this would 'strengthen the blood'.

One of Mam's most dubious cures came when Peter and I had whooping cough. Some roadmen were working near the entrance to Wilmot's field at the end of the row and had with them a vat of boiling tar that they were spreading on the footpath. Mam took us there, and after a word to the men, held us one by one over the steam. It was not the best of Mam's curative ideas; nevertheless the smell of tar still gives me an illogical feeling of being cosseted. For our cuts and abrasions, Mam bought a green ointment from the chemists', Zambuk, that was supposed to promote healing. She soothed our nettle stings by covering them with dock leaves.

But it was colds that prompted what I considered to be the best of Mam's cures: a concoction claiming to be a mixture of lemons and barley—'lemon barley water'—which tasted good, and at least gave us plenty of vitamin C. For sore throats she whipped butter and sugar together and presented it to us on a saucer. I suppose the butter tamed the soreness and the sugar promoted the body's own soothing secretions. We were not above faking a bad throat in order to get our butter and sugar treat.

As do most children after they begin school, Pete and I had constant colds, in addition to childhood diseases such as whooping cough, measles, chicken pox, and the flu. The doctor was a frequent visitor at our house, so much so that after a while he began to urge my parents to move us into the cleaner air of the hills.

Fortunately, Dad worked for a company that was part of a scheme, started in 1911 by David Lloyd George, in which a certain amount was deducted from his wages, and this, plus contributions from his employer and the government, meant that he could choose to be on a certain doctor's 'panel'. We were on Dr Anderson's, which meant that he would come to the house whenever my mother phoned him. We had one of the few phones in the village.

Dr Anderson, a small, grizzled Scotsman who was usually dressed in brown tweed, had his surgery in Green Lane, Belper. He had a reassuring bedside manner and was famous for prescribing something he called 'hot fomentations' for anything from boils to croup. The fomentation was a clay-like substance that he ordered Mam to warm in a saucepan and afterwards apply to my chest (or my boil) on a piece of flannel. Failing the fomentations, if I had a cold, the doctor instructed Mam to rub my chest nightly with something called camphorated oil that she bought from Boots, the chemist. It had a pungent smell that I suppose loosened my sinuses.

Dr Anderson also prescribed liquid medicines that were the colour of well-brewed tea. It was never clear what was in them, or even whether one medicine differed from another, but Dad usually picked them up for us after hours from a little shelf attached to the outside of the surgery door. The medicine came in a flat bottle with a cork in the neck and wrapped in white paper with 'Brenda Wallis, The Medicine' written on it. One my mother particularly approved of was 'The Tonic', a metallic-tasting concoction that probably had iron in it. I don't remember if it did me any good. An eight-ounce bottle cost a half-crown.

My most vivid memory of Dr Anderson was of his ministrations after I, aged five, had torn a piece of flesh from my left knee on the loose metal band of the half beer barrel Mam kept by the front door for her flowers. I was rushed off to the surgery, probably howling like a banshee. There wasn't a lot of blood, fortunately, and I had to wait my turn until Dr Anderson could deal with me. When the time came, I was ushered into his surgery where a bright fire glowed in the hearth. On the fire was a saucepan and in the boiling water the needles, scissors, and thread the doctor needed to sew up my wound. What can I say of the scene? I was given no anaesthetic, and Dad held me while Dr Anderson sewed, I screamed bloody murder, and the patients still in the waiting room looked gratifyingly alarmed when I finally made my exit. The missing piece of flesh was never found, and we all assumed that Peter the dog had eaten it.

Some time while we still lived at Ambergate, Dr Anderson took a partner, Dr Grey, a very different sort of man. He was younger than Dr Anderson and wore a tailcoat, which to my fascination he raised, one tail on each arm, as he stood luxuriously and decorously warming his bottom before the fire in my parents' bedroom where I usually spent my sick days. He also was much more of a dandy than Dr Anderson and, being an educated Englishman, had what my mother decided was a 'pound note' accent, rather like that of our neighbour, Mahster Donald's father, Mr Kay. When he first came to the house he got my mother's back up, probably because of his upper-class accent, so that she afterwards told Dr Anderson, 'Never send that man to my door again!' Even then, doctors were not the gods they sometimes think themselves to be, especially not to my mother. Dr Anderson, however, was not to be bullied. 'If the weans are ill and I cannae come, you'll have to have ma parrrtner,' he told Mam. She later came to like Dr Grey, although she was always more fond of Dr Anderson.

Dr Grey was more modern in his approach than his partner, and this was evident in his use of what to my ear he called 'the teblits', rather than liquid medicines. After he had been to see me, at the surgery door there would be waiting a little round pillbox with my name and 'The Tablets' written on the top. With liquid medicines I usually contrived to let some of it dribble down my chin, but tablets were much harder to deal with. Even so, they often ended up between my cheek and teeth until I could spit them down the lavatory when Mam wasn't looking. They probably did me just as much good that way as if I'd actually swallowed them. The same was probably true of 'The Medicine'.

Scarlet fever was a scourge at that time. We children were particularly afraid of catching it because, if you fell victim, you were sent to the Isolation Hospital on the hill above Ambergate. One village girl, also named Brenda, almost died of the disease, and I was distressed when I heard that the congregation at the church had mistakenly prayed for my soul rather than for hers. I spent a lot of time on my knees after that, pleading, 'They meant her, Lord. Not me!'

Of course, the greatest fear parents had in the '20s and '30s was that their children would be stricken with infantile paralysis, or polio as it was later called. A girl at Ambergate School had it and thereafter wore a brace on her shoulders. We children treated her with a kind of hands-off awe. She was not able to play and run about with the rest of us, and although she was never mocked, she was looked upon as a sort of oddity. I remember standing behind her in a queue and accidentally touching the lumps formed by the brace on her back. I was horrified and apologized, although I had done the girl no harm.

In the thirties, if children had what the doctor felt were too many sore throats, he would recommend that they have their tonsils out. It was a very common operation at the time. I was lucky, because this was when Dr Anderson advised Dad to move the family to the hills surrounding the valley. Dad was doing well in his work for General Refractories, garnering a lot of orders and a rise in pay, so that he was able to buy a half-acre of land in the little village of Fritchley in the hills above the Derwent Valley and begin to have a house built. The subsequent move seems to have done the trick as far as my tonsils were concerned, but Pete continued to have sore throats and swollen glands, until eventually he had to have his tonsils removed. That was when I began to doubt the benefit to me of our move to Fritchley, when Pete came home from the hospital and was fed, for what seemed like weeks, on ice cream. When I protested, Mam told me that I didn't need ice cream, not having had a tonsillectomy. To me, that was 'the most unkindest cut of all'.

CHAPTER 14

To Market, to Market!

BEFORE THE SECOND WORLD War, many tradesmen came to our door with their wares. Mr Knapp, the travelling salesman from Burgon's, a grocer's shop in Crown Square, Matlock, was a weekly visitor. He usually arrived in the evening carrying his attaché case, which he left open invitingly on the floor. It contained samples of the few packaged foods available at the shop. I don't remember Mam ever looking into it because she didn't believe in either packaged or tinned food; nevertheless, it was part of the salesman's ritual, and Peter, sliding about the floor on his chamber pot, was often the only one curious enough to have a look at his offerings. After greetings and the conveyance of any news he might have about mutual acquaintances in Matlock, Mr Knapp would take out his order book, and Mam listed her requirements; usually they were the same as those of the week before: sugar, tea, butter, cheese, lard, and bacon. Sometimes something called cream crackers would be added, which were a sore disappointment because they were actually water biscuits with not a trace of cream about them. Margarine was never ordered; Mam looked upon the spread with scorn. The box of groceries was delivered by van a couple of days later.

The local fishmonger, 'Fishy' Marsh, who had a shop on King Street in Belper, came on Fridays, driving his open-sided van with its pitched roof and sloping display counters where he had laid out the fish among ice shavings. Mr Marsh was an extremely large, fleshy man in a striped and bloodied fishy-smelling apron; Mam usually bought cod and herring from him, both of which were still plentiful. Dad liked his herrings 'soused' in vinegar and capers and then baked.

Twice a week we had a visit from the green grocer with his horse and cart. The grocer, Mr Wibberly, lived in what later became my brother Peter's house on Belper Road; he used the tiny shed on the roadside as his shop. Looking at it now, I can't imagine how the grocer made a living out of such a small space. He had his display shelves outside in clear weather, and people from the upper part of the village had to come down to shop; the Wibberly's horse wasn't capable of pulling the wagon up the very steep hill. Mr Wibberly was a lean, rather saturnine man usually dressed in a brown, coat-like overall; his horse, in summer, wore a straw hat with holes for its ears, along with a nosebag and blinkers to keep it from shying at the traffic on the A6. I would sometimes take it a dandelion, but it always seemed more interested in the contents of its bag.

The green grocer's offerings were not as varied as those of today. He stocked the usual local fruits, including apples, pears, blackberries, and strawberries in season, plus oranges and bananas from abroad. There were few exotic fruits except for the pineapples and the pomegranates, which we ate by picking out the red, flesh-covered seeds with a pin. Kiwis had not yet appeared in England, and we never saw kumquats or mangoes. The vegetable offerings were carrots, potatoes, onions, and turnips, and for green stuffs cabbage and Brussels sprouts. My father grew our lettuce, green runner beans, and peas; broccoli didn't come to his attention until after we moved to Fritchley.

The butcher, also from Belper, came with roasts and stew beef. I was not fond of meat and more often than not, Mam would save my midday stew and keep it congealing in the pantry. I had to eat it before I was allowed to have tea, our evening meal. (This was usually Dad's edict; if he was still at work, Mam often relented.)

A baker, whom we called 'the bread man', also called at the house, although my mother made most of our bread, pies, and cakes. In our village, bread was either homemade or baked by a local baker who produced either tall, white loaves with a good, firm crumb, or smaller brown ones called Hovis. I didn't like these as well as Mam's homemade bread, but they were better than the myriad choices of white, cushiony pap that is the norm today. Superior whole-wheat loaves that often contain all sorts of seed have overtaken Hovis.

Mr Wilmot, the milkman and Mickey's father, called each day with his horse and cart, and the coal man came periodically with his rattling flatbed truck with one-hundredweight hessian bags of coal stacked in the back. The coalman wore a leather apron that covered his clothes front and back, and a peaked cap worn backwards in order to protect his neck from the coal dust. After he had drawn up to our gate, with his back to the lorry, the man hoisted one of the open-topped bags onto his back, carried it down the entryway to our coalhouse, bent forward, and sent the coals cascading over his head to the floor with a great clatter. 'I hope there's no slack in there!' Mam would call from the house. 'Slack' was fine coal dust that refused to burn unless it had been cleaned. The coalhouse, which used to be outside the house and was later enclosed by a glass porch, was used by my mother in her last years as a cupboard for garden tools, ladders, and the like. By then, domestic coal fires were outlawed in many areas, and the fires along Matlock road were fuelled by gas.

All our food, most of which was bought in small quantities, was kept in the pantry. There were refrigerators then, but none of our neighbours owned one. We bought meat one day and ate it that day or the next; it was kept in a meat-safe, which at Ambergate was a birdcage-shaped affair with a ring handle at the top that was placed over the large platter that held the meat. At Fritchley the safe was a box with a mesh front and two shelves inside; the mesh was supposed to keep away the flies. Occasionally in hot weather, a roast developed a suspicious slipperiness, and when this happened Mam still used it but washed it first in vinegar. Also in hot weather, Mam stood the milk jug in a bowl containing cold water and covered it with muslin. Our windows did not have screens to keep out the flies, and Mam swatted any that entered the house with a rolled-up newspaper, or else trapped them with flypaper: long, sticky strips she hung from the ceiling where the trapped flies buzzed their way to death.

In the summer, the ice cream man came round with a large icebox attached to his bicycle. If he sold Wall's ice cream, letters on the side of his cart would exhort us to 'Stop Me and Buy One'. Ice cream was a treat, and on ice cream day, all the mothers would come out with the children at the sound of the ice cream man's bell: Mrs Chisnell and Audrey, Mrs Wright and her two children, Mrs Hurst and Rita, and Mrs Gratrix and Margaret. One dreadful day, my mother came out and bought only an empty ice cream cone for me. (We called them cornets.) Dr Anderson had decided that my constant sore throats were the result, not only of the local fogs, but the pernicious eating of ice cream. Mam filled the empty cornets with thick cold custard, and I had to make do with that. A man also came with a van containing some of the goods available at his hardware shop: paints, brushes, coalscuttles, kitchenware, nails, hammers, and the like.

Then, there were the gypsies. Mam had a profound suspicion of these folk, as did the other women on our row; locally, gypsies were suspected of being petty thieves. Mam had a 'pound of best steak' taken from her kitchen table one day when she was being less than her usual vigilant self, and she swore that gypsies had stolen it; Dad pointed out that the culprit might have been Peter the dog. In addition to iodine lockets, the gypsies also had clothes pegs for sale that they had whittled themselves, and Mam often bought a dozen or so.

I don't know if the gypsies were from what we called 'Rumania'; it is more likely they were so-called tinkers, that is, travelling people from Ireland. Unlike the gypsies of today, they usually travelled in the beautiful gypsy caravans one sees in illustrations in children's books, the wagons having elaborately carved doorways with coloured designs on them and steps that pulled down at the back. My Wallis grandmother was friendly with some of these people and occasionally took me to visit their encampment in a nearby quarry off Longway Bank. Granny was particularly friendly with an old matriarch who was usually to be found sitting on the steps of her caravan smoking a pipe. I have no idea how Granny had met the gypsy woman, although these were not wandering gypsies and had been settled in the cupola yard for some years; their children had attended the school at Whatstandwell. Perhaps the old lady had been there when Granny was a girl, and they had known each other then. The name of the gypsy family was Smith.

In addition to all these services, a knife grinder sometimes came down the road with his grinding wheel attached to his bicycle, and now and again a rag-and-bone man appeared with his cry of 'Ragsabones!' He collected our old clothes, if we had any, to sell to the poor, but I doubt he found anyone with bones to give him. No one seemed to know what he would do with them, except perhaps take them to a glue factory. In the thirties at least eight tradesmen came to our door; today, only milk is delivered, and in many places not even that.

As well as travelling tradesmen, there were various shops and businesses in the village. Opposite the Hurt Arms was Tritton's sweetshop in a wooden shack, and on the Ripley corner a petrol station run by Mr Waddington, Jean's father. Opposite this garage, in the car park for The Hurt Arms, a small, two-story gritstone building housed a blacksmith's forge, where local farmers and people staying at the pub took their horses to be shod. Occasionally, as we passed the forge, if the blacksmith was working at his anvil, Mam and I would linger a moment to watch. Even though Mam held tightly to my hand, I found the forge both exciting and frightening. The room was a dark cave where the only light came from a blazing fire near which a great horse stood, impatiently clattering its great hooves on the stone floor, while a huge sweating man clad in rough work clothes and a leather apron hammered a piece of red-hot metal into the shape of a horseshoe. On many days when I was playing in the garden, I heard the *chink, chink* of the blacksmith's hammer against the shoe he was shaping, and shivered. Even in the thirties and forties, horses were still a useful means of getting about, not only on farms but also for hauling goods short distances. Through the war years, when petrol was scarce, shire horses clattered about hauling drays loaded with beer kegs to the local pubs.

Further along the village, just beyond the church, the Promenade Cafeand petrol station was kept by a little man my parents called 'Winky Woo' after some comic character of the day. He was very small, almost a dwarf, and rode an adult tricycle, but his fascination for me was that he kept a pet monkey. The animal was usually on a leash, crouching on the top of a petrol pump, although sometimes it rode round the village perched on the back of Winky Woo's bike. Further still along the village was a hairdresser's and near the White Hart pub a flurry of shops: a general store, a butcher's, a stationer's, a sweet shop, and a fish and chip shop. The post office was up a road off the A6 (today it is on the main road), and the last shop in the village was Wibberly's green grocery.

When occasionally we ran out of some item, such as flour or sugar, Mam and I visited one of these little shops 'on the village'. In those days, sugar came in large barrels, as did flour, while rice was delivered in hefty hessian bags. If Mam wanted a pound or so of sugar, the shopkeeper used a metal scoop to remove it from its barrel before pouring it into the pan of the weighing machine and from there into a blue paper bag. Bags for sugar were always blue. Similarly, rice or flour was weighed and put into a bag, usually a white one. Even biscuits were 'loose', that is, not in packages or ornate boxes, but sitting in bins with glass lids, allowing the customers to choose a variety. These, too, the owner weighed and put into a bag.

Butter came as a block and not as four sticks in a box, and when Mam ordered a pound, the man cut a slab from the block, placed it on a wooden board, and patted it into shape using two wooden paddles that he had previously dipped in water. Sometimes he 'prettied up' the block using a mould that produced a pattern depicting a sheaf of wheat or a cow on the top surface of the butter. Margarine had an unpleasant taste then and was scorned by many housewives of the time.

Mam stowed all these purchases in the shopping basket she carried over her arm. There was much less packaging in the thirties, and consequently much less litter in the streets. Later, during the war, we learned to save paper and cardboard and our few tin cans and allowed the railings outside our houses to be sawn off and used for making armaments. (Or so we were told. The paper and cardboard were used, but recently I learned that we sacrificed our railings in vain; their final resting place being either the bottom of Thames estuary or of the Firth of Forth. Possibly someone discovered, too late, that such metal was useless in the making of arms.)

In addition to all these village businesses, there was WH Smith's bookstall at the station, on what is now the only remaining platform, where for a few pence Dad could rent a book for a week or so, or buy a daily paper or a paperback. He often brought books home from the station, and as I became older, I read them too: AJ Cronin, Dorothy Sayers, and Marjorie Allingham, but this was later when I was twelve and we had moved to Fritchley.

Today in the village the bookstall is no longer there, nor is the green grocer's or the stationer's. Only one of the petrol stations remains, in addition to the general store and the butcher's shop. Even so, Ambergate has not become as bereft of local outlets as has many another village.

CHAPTER 15
Off to School!

Ambergate School

I WAS FIVE WHEN I first went to Ambergate School, which was then (and remains today) a red brick building halfway up Toadmoor Road. My mother and Mrs Hurst took Rita and me to school that first morning and put us into the capable hands of our teacher, Miss Beecham, the large, red-faced country-woman, the one who taught me the Lord's Prayer. The first morning consisted of kindergarten (then called 'The Babies'), where we, for some reason the only beginners that day, were introduced to a doll's house. Neither of us had seen anything that grand in our lives. There were many rooms and lots of furniture, but no dolls. Rita and I played desultorily with it, placing the small chairs and sofas here and there, but without dolls to people it, the house seemed rather pointless. We went home for dinner in the middle of the day and afterwards were escorted back to begin learning in earnest; it seemed that kindergarten was over.

At school that afternoon and on subsequent days we began learning our letters, how to form them and the sounds they made, followed later by simple sentences of 'The cat sat on the mat' variety. In a short while, I had my hands on what became one of my greatest pleasures in life. I had wanted to read long before I was old enough for school, and family legend has it that at the age of three, I was once found sitting in front of my play cupboard reading a book and exclaiming 'Ho, said the Prectus!' Neither I nor anyone else could explain what a Prectus was; moreover, so I've been told, the book was upside-down.

In learning to read, of course, I also learned to write and after moving up into the next class, I was awarded my first literary prize. It was for a short story, probably a very short one. The teacher, a Mr Prasher from Matlock, had wrung my heart when he told us about the plight of pit ponies that were then in use at local mines to pull the heavy coal wagons to the lifts. The poor creatures never saw the light of day and usually died in the mine. My story began, 'There he was at the bottom of the pit.' (I'm rather proud of that *in medias res* beginning.)

It went on to chronicle the life of a pit pony and its subsequent rescue by a kind miner who bought its release from the mine so that it could spend its declining years among the

Boys with Pit Pony

flowers of a meadow. My prize was an apple and a new penny. Pennies, until the sixties or seventies, were made of copper and an inch or so across; when new they shone like gold and were greatly prized by us children. That day I ran all the way home to show my prize to Mam.

Unfortunately, when I began to form my letters and also when I learned to sew, Miss Beecham, appalled to find that I did both left-handed, insisted that I use my right. This went on for some time, I getting more and more agitated, so much so that after a while my mother, greatly daring since parents then had very little clout with teachers, came to the school to protest. Miss Beecham relented, but perhaps as a result of her prior insistence that I use my right hand, I am now ambidextrous: I write with my left hand, but I sew with my right.

Lois Lee, an older girl who lived in a house opposite No. 5, was my escort to school in the very early days. Later, Margaret, having started school a year ahead of me, became my companion along with Rita. Each morning, my mother, Mrs Hurst, or Mrs Gratrix escorted us as far as the crossroads at the Hurt Arms Hotel and saw us across the busy Ripley Road, after which we walked the rest of the way by ourselves. Only a few families had a car and we all lived nearby, which meant that everyone walked to school.

Margaret and I were still best friends, and it was she who protected us from the school bully, Dennis Campbell, who lived near Wilmot's farm in a large, red brick house. Dennis was truly a menace, following us the whole way home, punching and pinching us, or threatening to do so. Rita and I were terrified of him. Margaret, however, had learned a thing or two from her father, and one day we were on our way home when Dennis ran up and began hitting us. Margaret had had enough. 'Here, hold these!' She thrust her glasses at me and began punching Dennis back as hard as she could, doing so much damage to him that his father complained about it to Mr Gratrix. He left us alone after that.

Tritton's sweet shop, opposite the Hurt Arms near the space now occupied by a little restaurant, was a Mecca for both Margaret and me. Occasionally we were given a penny or so to spend at the shop. Once, egged on by Margaret, I stole three ha'pennies from my mother's purse and spent them on treats for us on the way to school. Mr Tritton, an old friend of my father's, innocently mentioned my purchases to Mam and got me into hot water.

Usually we bought long black strings of liquorice, which we called 'bootlaces', and often some sort of fizzy, coloured powder that bubbled up in its three-cornered paper package when we added water. Bull's Eyes and Liquorice Allsorts were also favourites. Once, in summer, when Mr Tritton was cleaning out his icebox, he gave Margaret a 'snowball', after which we ran as fast as we could towards school to show our prize. It had melted long before we reached it.

Apart from the sad life of pit ponies and the three Rs—reading, writing, and religion—I can't remember much more that I learned at Ambergate School. Sewing lessons, which came up weekly, didn't turn me into a seamstress. We were supposed to learn hemming and were given a scrap of material and a needle and thread, and left to get on with it. This was good practice except that at the end of the lesson, all the scraps were tossed into a large hamper, and the next week we were supposed to recognize our own handiwork, take it from the hamper, and work on it again. Many times I was unable to find my scrap and so spent the lesson pretending to sew the hem of my skirt. Once I made an apron with much help from Mam. It was brown with an embroidered orange border, and I thought it very handsome. I must have learned some maths, because I could at least count, add, subtract, and multiply by the time I left the school at the age of eight.

Although I hadn't noticed, Mam was pregnant again, and one terrible night in 1936 with much moaning and no comforting anaesthetics, she produced my sister Beryl. It was a terrible night for me, too. I was just eight years old and knew nothing of reproduction, despite the fact that I was a country girl and no stranger to farms. I knew only that Mam was confined to her bed and that terrible sounds were coming from her room.

My Grandmother Durward came and put me to bed, giving no satisfactory replies to my anxious questions of 'What's wrong with Mammy?' My father, like most fathers then, had taken himself off to the Hurt Arms to be out of the way. For hours I lay rigidly in my bed in the little box room, awful wails and sometimes screams echoing from my mother's room and people coming and going. Nervously, I crept out from time to time to ask again, 'What's wrong with Mammy?', but still no one would give me an explanation. Mam's door was firmly closed. Where was Peter, I wonder now?

At last, after hours of terror, the sounds from the next room ceased, and I ventured out onto the landing once more to peek through my mother's door that was now standing open. She was lying on her side being swabbed down by Mrs Wilmot who, on seeing me, immediately covered her with a sheet. 'Bren!' Mam said, her voice weak, 'Come and say hello to your sister.' And there was Beryl, a beautiful baby. Trembling, I gave my sister her first kiss and afterwards, limp with relief, let Mrs Wilmot usher me back to bed. 'Of course,' I told myself, 'it must have been the baby I heard!' Thus comforted, I fell deeply asleep.

It was shortly after this that our family numbers jumped from five to six when my mother's sister, Aunt Gladys, came to live with us to help with the baby. Gladys was very young at the time, short, with wavy brown hair and intense blue eyes like her mother's. We were to become good friends. A small vignette that sticks in my mind for no apparent reason: shortly after she joined the family, Gladys is standing on a chair in our back room putting something onto the top shelf of a cupboard. 'How old are you, Gladys?' I ask.

'Eighteen,' she replies. How old she seems! I tell her that I am eight.

Gladys and Peter now occupied the back bedroom, Mam, Dad, and the baby the front one, and I was still in my box room. The little house was bursting at the seams, so change was inevitable, and soon. Dr Anderson had continued to urge my father to get his sickly family out of the valley, and by the time of Beryl's birth, the house Dad had commissioned to be built on the half acre he had bought in Fritchley was near completion. Gladys called it the House that Jack Built.

To me, Ballantrae House seemed huge, almost as large as The Beeches, my grandparents' old house. It was built of brick and had a sizeable entrance hallway with a beautiful tiled floor done in a pattern of medallions in black, cream, and blue. There, we put the telephone on the wall and a large coat stand in one corner. The windows of the front porch included what Mam called 'me lights': stained glass windows, which for her meant that, socially, she had arrived. The sitting room had a big bay window, again with 'lights', overlooking the front garden, and a small one at the side with a view towards Ripley.

Apart from the fact that it had no bay windows, the dining room was a mirror image of the sitting room; both rooms had tiled fireplaces. The kitchen was across the hallway, directly facing the front door, and contained a hatch in the shape of a large cupboard with glass doors on both the kitchen and dining room sides where dishes could be passed through. They never were. There was also a gas stove, sink, and a fireplace with a side oven. The old table from 5, Matlock Road sat under the window that looked out to the back garden. A small pantry led off the kitchen, and the back door opened onto an enclosed hallway where there was a coalhouse, a separate lavatory, and a small room that housed the gas meter.

Upstairs were four bedrooms, three large ones and a smaller one that Dad used as his office. There was also a bathroom with a separate lavatory and a box room. The garage was under one of the bedrooms. After Matlock Road, Ballantrae House seemed to me a palace.

While the house was being built, Margaret and I often walked up through the fields and the Top Hag in order to check on the workmen's progress and to see how the gardener was getting on. The garden had been a field and was full of twitch-grass and small stones, so the man Dad hired to make it into a garden had a difficult job. He was tall, and I thought quite old—his hair was white—and he wore corduroy trousers with strings tied about the knees and a bandanna round his neck. He worked tirelessly, but neither the garden nor the house were quite complete when Dad decided it was time to get ourselves together for the move up the hill to Fritchley. Our Ambergate house was rented out; we were to keep ownership of it until my mother's death almost sixty years later.

I had been a happy child at No. 5, Matlock Road and will always be grateful for that happiness. A child can have no greater gift from his or her parents. Nevertheless, in the autumn of 1937 when I was nine and set off to help Aunt Gladys wheel Beryl in her pram along the Ripley Road and up Bullbridge Hill to our new house in Fritchley, I left my old home behind without a backward glance.

PART 2

1937–1951

Fritchley Green

CHAPTER 16

We Take to the Hills

WHEN WE MOVED TO Fritchley, there were six of us: Mam, Dad, Gladys, Peter, Beryl, and me. At the time, we three children were a little younger than we are in the photograph: I was nine, Pete four, and Beryl just a baby of a few months. Photographs of any sort were in short supply in those days; my parents had a camera that worked only intermittently, and studio photographs, like this one, were too expensive to indulge in often.

Initially, the move to Fritchley was a happy one for me, until the day I went to school and found myself voted 'posh' by the village children. The label put quite a crimp in my social life. In Ambergate, posh had been what we had called children like Master Donald and Miss Sarah, whose accents were much more 'pound note' than our own. Now, however, I had to face the fact that because my family lived in a house rather larger than theirs, and owned a car and a telephone, my new school-mates found me a step or two above them on the social ladder. Other drawbacks were that my father's job didn't involve the coalface, a lime quarry, an assembly line, or a farm; worse, even though our accents 'sounded Derbyshire', they were not quite as broad as those of my fellow pupils. It was as though the Fritchley children thought I had done this on purpose to one-up them. Nevertheless, I had to admit we were suddenly of a higher class than we had been in Ambergate, and there was no escaping it. When I complained at home, my father laughed and told me that he didn't expect to be accepted at his new pub, the King's Arms, for at least ten years. I was not amused. In my opinion, grownups were not as merciless to newcomers as were children.

Fritchley, it turned out, was different from Ambergate in several other ways. To begin with, it was much older. While Ambergate had grown up around the railway as recently as the 1840s, Fritchley had farms that dated back to the seventeenth century; even earlier the area had been under Roman occupation, and there were traces of their lead mines at nearby Crich.

The village is spread over a bowl-shaped depression on a hillside to the north of the River Amber and east of the Derwent, its northern border contiguous with the southern

border of Crich. From the Crich Common Road, Fritchley Lane swoops down past a stone farmhouse, rows of cottages, a chapel, the school, and a pub to the village green with its red telephone box. Gritstone cottages surround the green, along with the square block of the Congregational Chapel and, in the 1930s, a general grocery and a butcher's shop. Allen Lane, a second entrance into the village from lower down the Common Road, meets Fritchley Lane at the village green, after which Fritchley Lane swings left, passing a Quaker Meeting House, a few houses, and the post office. Allen Lane, then swings right, passing a pub and more stone cottages until, as one, the two roads join to sweep down steep Bobbin Mill Hill to bottom out at Fritchley Brook. From there the road swoops up again to an area called The Dimple, which has more stone cottages and ancient farmhouses. Fields and woods surround the village, and to the northwest, reached by Chadwicknick Lane where we lived stretch the gritstone Tors where discarded millstones that the farmers used for milling their grain still lay unused among the grasses.

The houses in our old village had been predominantly redbrick with just an odd gritstone house or cottage here and there. Fritchley had mostly ancient lime and gritstone cottages with red brick showing up in the council houses and in the more elaborate dwellings of the well-to-do. Many of the latter were at the higher end of the village, near where our new house stood.

In earlier days, Fritchley had industries such as a corn mill at Mill Green and a bobbin mill at the lower end of the village. Before Arkwright revolutionized cotton spinning, a cottage industry had developed in the village where women spun and weaved at home, while the men not involved in farming went to Crich to work in the lime quarry or the kilns at Ambergate. By the time we moved to Fritchley, the corn mill was closed, the bobbin mill had burned down, and the young women rode busses into Belper or Lea Bridge every morning to work in shops, or at Strutt's or Smedley's cotton mills, or walked down to Bullbridge to work at the dye works. The men were often colliers in the mines at Ripley, quarry workers in nearby Crich, or workmen at the limekilns or the dye works. It was an easy matter to deduce where some of them made their living: by the end of their shifts, the hair of the mill girls was thick with cotton fuzz, the miners' eyes gleamed huge in their coal-blackened faces, and those who worked in the limestone quarries or at the kilns had frosted eyebrows and a layer of white dust in their hair. There were no pit baths until later, and the workers had to clean up at home. One housewife I knew, who lived in one of the cottages in Fritchley Lane, always had a large tin bath sitting before the fire and kettles heating up when her husband came home. When he entered and dropped his snap bag onto the floor, it was time for the children to make themselves scarce and for the miner to climb out of his coal-stiffened clothes and into the steaming water. Pithead baths, when they were introduced, must have been a relief to the workman and particularly to his wife.

In addition to these working men and women, Fritchley had a few 'nobs' thrown in for ballast: people who owned the dye works at Bullbridge, one or two bankers, ministers for the local chapel and the church, two commercial travellers, and the Headmaster of the school.

We had hardly moved into our new home before Mam announced that it was time for Pete and me to go to school. I was indignant. I had believed that the move would include at least a week's holiday in order to get settled; it had not occurred to me that Mam would whisk us off to school the Monday after Friday's move.

She took us down to the school that first morning. The building belonged to the Church of England, as did many elementary schools of the time, so that the sandstone schoolhouse, shaped like a church, but without a steeple, doubled as a church on Sundays. It has since become a private house, most of its arched windows modernized.

The 'big room', for the oldest children, ages eight to fourteen, had a vaulted, nave-like ceiling and Gothic-shaped windows of plain glass, their sills crammed with what turned out to be huge ostrich egg shells. The room was heated by a coal stove that sat beside one of the long walls near the Headmaster's desk. Despite the stove's size, children sitting in the back rows often shivered with cold, their fingers and lips blue. Hot water pipes, heated by the stove, had to remove the chill from the big room as well as the other two classrooms. That first morning, when my brother and I were introduced to our teachers, we found that Peter was to be in the 'babies' class with Miss Outram. A sturdy boy, Pete had dark brown hair and eyes like those of Grandfather Wallis. His large, curved nose had a dip in it near where it met his forehead that had been caused when he fell onto an upturned bucket.

I was assigned to the big room under the eye of the Head. At nine, I was one of the youngest in the class. The eldest were hulking youths of almost fourteen, the age at which most of them would soon finish their education and follow their fathers into the mines or onto the farms, while the girls followed their mothers into the jobs those women had held before they married: in shops, the cotton mills, or the dye works.

When we arrived home from school that afternoon, Mam asked me how the day had gone, to which I grumped, 'All right'. I didn't tell her that the girls had ignored me, and that one girl had whispered to another, 'Let's send 'er to Cuventry'.

Fritchley School and Church

I had no idea what Cuventry was, and in any case, wanted no part of it. The boys hadn't spoken to me at all, but had fallen about, nudging one another and spluttering behind their hands as if there were something odd about me. I was furious; my friends at Ambergate hadn't been like that! No doubt this had been because our parents knew one another and we were all pretty much of the same class, but at nine this didn't occur to me, and I was bewildered and hurt. Finally, after my ostracism had gone on for a while with no improvement, I began to make attempts to blend in, dropping my aitches about me like confetti and using broader dialect words. One day I told a particularly bothersome boy to 'clear off, you daft sod', at which he shook his head in reproof. 'Yo munna talk broad', he admonished me seriously, 'your muther would'na like it!' ('You mustn't talk in dialect; your mother wouldn't like it'.) He was right about that. For what to me seemed like weeks, I continued to stand forlorn at the side of the schoolyard during the ten-thirty playtime and sit mute at my desk in the classroom. Meanwhile, Pete fit into his class like a ball slapping into a fielder's palm and was soon larking about with the other youngsters and talking as 'broad' as his new friends.

As time went by—possibly it was only a month, although to me it felt much longer—the girls gradually began to accept me. Probably the other children had been waiting for me to try to show my superiority in some way, but I was far too shy to attempt any such thing. I felt far from superior, and these children appeared to be much more in charge than I.

A change began to emerge one playtime after we were given the usual watery mixture of a drink called Horlicks that we always drank grudgingly. We had Horlicks at home, but our mothers usually made it with milk and we enjoyed it; made with water, we thought it disgusting. One morning as we sipped our beverage, a girl named Molly looked at me, wrinkled her nose, and pretended to gag. I laughed and did the same. Soon, all the girls were sipping their Horlicks and clutching their stomachs as though about to be sick. They looked at each other—miraculously they even looked at me—and laughed, sipped, and gagged. I joined in. It was clear, both that we all hated Horlicks and that the ice had begun to shift. A huge wave of relief engulfed me as I realized that I might finally become one of the gang.

What also helped in this detente is that Mam asked Mrs Rollinson, a neighbour who lived near us in Chadwicknick Lane, if their daughter, Jean, would walk Pete and me to school after that first morning. Jean was thirteen and had some standing at school, especially among the younger girls.

Mrs Rollinson had four children: Jean Barber and her older sister Joyce, the children of her first marriage, and Sheila and David, the children of her second. Jean's father had been a miner, and sometime after he was killed in the mine, his widow had married his friend, Frank Rollinson, who also worked in the pit. He was a large, friendly man whose nose and forehead, even after he had scrubbed his face at the sink amid much sloshing about of soap and water, was still pockmarked with the coal dust that had penetrated his skin. I was fascinated; he was the first miner I had seen close to.

The six of them lived happily though noisily together in their little house, and each morning Pete and I stepped into a scene of chaos when we arrived to call for our escort. Often, the two youngest children would still be in bed and Mrs Rollinson's plaintive cries of 'Shei-la, Da-vid! Come on!' would be echoing up the stairs. If Mr Rollinson were not on his shift at the mine, he usually added to the cacophony by yelling up the stairs in counterpoint to his wife and grumbling at his two older daughters. They called their stepfather Frank and gave back as good as they got. I knew that when David and Sheila finally made an appearance, there would be the washing ritual at the kitchen sink, first face, neck, and hands, followed by legs and feet. Meanwhile, the two Barber girls, who at thirteen and fourteen seemed to me like young women, were jockeying for space before the one mirror over the fireplace, where they primped for what seemed to me like hours. It was probably only about five minutes or so, but I was what we would call now an A-personality child and was terrified of being late for school.

After the ablutions it was time for a cooked breakfast involving bacon or sausage and eggs. By the time we left for school, I was usually in a panic, although we almost always arrived at school just as some child began to ring the big hand bell to summon us to Morning Prayer. 'There you are!' Jean would tell me comfortingly, giving me a small shove. 'What were you whittling about?'

Apart from having to overcome the drawback of my accent, there were also my clothes. Not that they were particularly fancy, but there was quite a lot of poverty in Fritchley in the thirties, much more so than in Ambergate. The miners and quarry workers, for example, were not at all well paid, as they were to become in the '70s before Margaret Thatcher put the mines out of business. Many of the children were dressed as well as I, especially if their mothers were members of the Women's Institute, who were often accomplished seamstresses. But some of the girls from the poorer families had to wear their older sisters' cast-offs, and some of the boys wore hand-me-downs from their fathers or older brothers, the coats and trousers cobbled together to fit their smaller frames. None of them went barefoot, although children sometimes had to wear outgrown shoes, their young toes bunching tighter and tighter together as they grew, their heels a mass of blisters. Shoes were also handed down from older siblings, so that many children from those times must still live with feet crippled by being forced into someone else's shoes.

Poverty also led to illness. Apart from some malnutrition here and there, and the usual colds, flu, measles, and chicken pox, there was tuberculosis in the village. (We called it consumption.) The mother of one classmate was wasting away with the disease when I was at school and died shortly after I left for my secondary school. In my father-in-law's day, there were still huts in many village gardens where the sufferers were confined so that their families might be spared the disease.

Hygiene was quite primitive in many houses in that part of the village, known locally as 'dahn Fritch'. Here, some of the houses lacked a bathroom, and the lavatories were earth closets across the yard. There was no domestic central heating then, and few people owned a telephone and even fewer a car. On the other hand, most of us who lived 'up Fritch' had bathrooms and indoor toilets in addition to cars and telephones. There is no wonder I was viewed as posh, and why I caused hilarity when I asked innocently, 'What are night soil men?' After much giggling and guffawing, I was informed that they were the men who drove their truck round the village at night, emptying the earth closets.

It was a great relief to me when I began to be accepted by the girls in my class. One in particular, Joan Barber (related to Jean, though I don't remember how) became a particular friend. She was a tiny girl, much shorter than the rest of us of a comparable age, with fair curls, blue eyes, and an extremely husky voice. I was devastated when Joan was run over by a car shortly after she and her family moved to Ambergate. I often think of her when we pass the cemetery where she was buried just to the north of Belper.

Molly continued to be friendly. She lived in a large stone house at the top of Bobbin Mill Hill, and had a mentally troubled sister who was never mentioned and seldom seen, although she too lived at the house. Whenever Molly invited me home, I was conscious of puzzling sounds coming from another room. Molly never gave me an explanation, but another girl told me that Molly had a handicapped sister, although she didn't use that phrase.

And there was Elizabeth, the butcher's daughter, who later became a friend when we both went to the same grammar school. Before that, however, I felt 'Lib' was particularly suspicious of me; she had been one of the girls who had sent me to Coventry for a while, and it took some time before she lost her fear that I might try to lord it over her. Elizabeth lived on the Green with her parents, two sisters, Mary and Margaret, and a brother, Fred.

Even after the group accepted me, playtime could still be an ordeal because, after we had drunk our watery Horlicks, no matter what the weather, we were expected to go outside 'to get some fresh air'. Our playground was no rich child's play space with slides and swings and places to scramble, but merely a yard like that at Ambergate School: a stretch of asphalt where we ran screaming in games of tag, skipped rope, or stood in groups, gossiping. The toilets were earth closets and woe betide the girl who had to 'go' during playtime, because boys sometimes climbed to the outhouse roof, removed a strategically loosened tile, peered down, and told their pals the colour of the girl's knickers. Usually the boys played together: fighting, yelling, and tormenting some of the slower children, or sometimes playing marbles. The girls usually went in for quieter games. When skipping, we chanted: 'My mother said/That I never should/Play with the gypsies/In the wood.'

Our worlds, the boys' and the girls', were usually quite separate, but occasionally the boys would invade the girls' territory. Jack, an older boy who had lived in Canada for a while, was much more sexually adventurous than the other children, and often decided he had to kiss some girl, or else egged on another boy to 'go on, kiss 'er'. I was sometimes the target. Many of the older youths in the school often hinted at more sophisticated sexual exploits, although even then I suspected that most of them were 'more say than do'. One of them, a farmer's son, brought a doughnut-shaped potato to school, along with an elongated one, which he proceeded to fit together in a suggestive way behind the Headmaster's back. By then I knew what he meant.

At Fritchley School what I learned, and retained, was history. The Headmaster was keen on two things: mental arithmetic and local history. 'Eight times four plus six minus two plus twenty-four,' he would cry, and there were always some waving hands, mine seldom among them; I was totally at sea. There was no one at home to help: Dad was busy; Mam had finished school at fourteen and could scarcely add; remedial classes were unheard of. The move from Ambergate to Fritchley means that my math skills today are rudimentary. I can add, subtract, and multiply (thank goodness for that rote learning, and later my grammar school years), but I have to pause and get a piece of paper if I have to work out percentages, and as for algebra or anything more abstruse, I'm lost. I was good at geometry, probably because it was based on accepted theorems that seemed to me to have some logic to them; enigmas such as $x + y = z$ had none. I enjoyed the history lessons, perhaps because real history was often punctuated with fascinating myths: King Alfred and the cakes; King Arthur and Camelot; King Knute ordering the waves to retreat. Among more authentic stories were, for example, King Harold's dying with an arrow through his eye at the battle of Hastings, or Queen Boadicea (Boudicca nowadays) attaching knives to the wheels of her chariot in order to make mincemeat of the Romans.

Local history also involved lectures from the teacher on such subjects as Mary Queen of Scots' imprisonment at Wingfield Manor, which was two miles away, or of Cromwell's rampage through the county in the 1640s. The Headmaster informed us that Chadwicknick Lane, where our house stood, had been named for one of Cromwell's captains, who spent the night bivouacked with his men in what is still a farmer's field. He pointed out the stone troughs where Chadwick had watered his horses, after which he and his soldiers galloped over the hill to attack Wingfield Manor, where Royalist forces were gathering.

Wingfield Manor (John Grain)

We also learned about Arkwright and Jedediah Strutt and their cotton mills, the building of the canals by Dutchmen imported to do the work, the history of the mines and quarries around us, and of Stephenson's small railways that carried limestone from the Hilt's and Crich quarries, through Fritchley and down to the limekilns at Ambergate.

One large plus—although I didn't think it a plus at the time—was that the Church of England was in charge of Fritchley School, and consequently we spent a considerable time reading the King James Bible. Every morning before playtime at 10.30, we ploughed our way through Genesis, Exodus, and the Psalms. We even read the Begats, and of course the New Testament. Through the King James Bible, I learned the beauty of the English language; today, the newer translations strike my ears as oddly flat.

Since this was a church school, periodically the school governors came to quiz us on what we had learned from our religious instruction. The advent of these men made the teachers jittery, and they passed their nervousness on to us. The Head was particularly apprehensive, and his cane became even more in evidence as the day approached. He was in the habit of caning the boys (seldom the girls), especially if they were slow or 'cheeked' him, but when the governors were on the horizon, he became ferocious. 'Fetch Little Willie!' he would command some offending boy. Little Willie was the Head's name for his cane. After the boy had delivered his weapon to the Head, he was ordered to hold out his hand to receive six blows to his palm. Often the boy singled out would be backward, such as one who was reputed to be 'nine pence to the shilling'. (The last time I saw him, a few years ago, he was driving his own Rolls Royce. Perhaps he had been a full bob, after all.)

In the 1930s, we were still very close to the Great War, and on November 11th we celebrated Remembrance Day at Fritchley School, as we had at Ambergate. Before the ceremony the Headmaster, who had fought in the trenches during the war and been badly gassed, indicated to us the horrors of it all, not in specific detail, but so that I remember quite clearly his distress. For me, John McCrae's lines evoked the same feeling: 'In Flanders fields the poppies blow/Between the crosses, row on row'.

Unfortunately, the Head had another trait: he liked children, boys or girls, and the older children, especially the boys, soon 'twigged' just how much he liked them. The Headmaster had a habit, when one of us approached to ask a question, of inviting the child to come closer and stand behind his desk. Then, with one hand held over the wrist of the other, he would flap it in the direction of the child's genitals. The boys had developed a signal of warning and mockery: one wrist over the other, the hand flapping frantically. I once approached the Head's desk and was invited to stand behind it, close to his chair. We talked, the hand flapped, but did not touch me; however, I gradually became aware that a couple of the older boys were gesturing and murmuring something obviously directed at me. One of the boys was openly making the flapping-hand signal; I was being warned. Not really knowing what I was being warned against—I believe I thought the flapping hand might eventually slap me—I stepped away from the desk. Some years later, after I had left for grammar school, the Head transferred to a job elsewhere and was soon dismissed for 'interfering' with children. He committed suicide shortly thereafter. My Grandmother Wallis, who had known him in his youth, told me sadly, 'Poor man. He was gassed in the War, you know.' She was probably not fully aware of what he had done, although for her generation it was sufficient to know that if a man had been in the trenches in France he should be forgiven just about any transgression.

Another class I enjoyed was art. Miss Palliser, a tall, horsey-looking woman who lived at Ludlow's, the Quaker Guest House, during term time, was the teacher for the class that came between the babies and the big room and taught art to the school in general. The class had nothing to do with the lives or the production of actual artists, but was an opportunity for us children to draw or to mess about with paints. The colours delighted us. A child named Seton, son of a local miner, when splashing colour onto his paper, said delightedly, 'Look, deep pairple.' Everyone knew what he meant: 'Deep Purple' was the popular song of the moment: 'When the deep purple falls/Over dreamy garden walls/And the stars begin to flicker in the sky.' Jean Barber took up the song. She had what we all thought was 'a nice voice' and took lessons from a teacher at Bullbridge. 'Have you heard Deena Durbin?' she asked. (In Fritchley, Deana was known as 'Deena'.) Everyone except me had heard her on the wireless or seen her at 'the pictures' in Crich; she was the latest singing sensation.

One of Jean Barber's passions was what we called 'passy partoo', which was popular with many children of the time. There were several examples of her work on the Rollinson's walls. To make a passé partout picture, Jean would take a piece of black construction paper, cut out the silhouette of a woman dressed in a poke bonnet and a hoop skirt, and afterwards fill in the outline of her dress with the silver paper wrappings from chocolates, cigarettes, and the like. Afterwards she sandwiched the colourful result between two sheets of glass and fastened them together with passé partout, a sort of black, sticky tape. I was most impressed; the only use I had found for the silver paper that wrapped Dad's cigarettes or the tangerines at Christmas was to fashion small wine glasses from it for my doll.

Every year, a visiting nurse, sent by the local authorities, came to the school to check on our health and make sure the one or two vaccines of the time were up-to-date. She checked us for head lice, and I was astonished one day when she quietly took me aside to whisper that I should mention to my mother that she had found what we called 'nits' among my hair. I noticed that she didn't whisper when conveying the same message to the more working-class children. After I informed Mam of my infestation, she spent at least a half hour a day combing through my hair with a 'nit comb' and cracking her resulting haul between her thumbnails.

Among the boys in my class at school was a little fellow who sat in front of me. He had fair hair, very pink cheeks, and large green eyes. He was clever and quiet and was seldom in trouble with the Head like many of the other boys, except for an incident when the Head yelled at him because he continued to insist that his spelling of 'worter' was the correct one. I liked him for his quietness and the fact that he never teased me. His name was

Joe Smith, and he came from Barn Close Farm just outside the village. His mischievous younger brother, who was also at the school, was usually referred to as 'that Tommy Smith'; he was in the babies' class when I first arrived at Fritchley.

Joe Smith at Barn Close Farm

Barn Close Farm, Fritchley

The school's library consisted of one low bookcase containing at most thirty books, among them Susan Coolidge's Katydid series—*What Katy Did at School; What Katy Did Next*—and LM Montgomery's *Ann of Green Gables* and *Ann of Avon Lea*. I had never had access to so many books at one time, and I gobbled them up. At home we had a Pear's Encyclopedia that we called 'Uncle Jackie's book' because we had borrowed it from my uncle years before; Dad used it occasionally to help with his crossword puzzles. The only other books in the house were the mysteries Dad brought home from WH Smith's lending library on Ambergate station. My mother never took me to a library, perhaps because the nearest county library was then at Derby (where I was to be junior librarian some years later), and in any case she was already worried by my love of reading. 'Bren, you'll wreck your eyes!' was her constant warning. Boots, the chemists, had a lending library, but it too was in Derby, and there was no local library at either Belper or Matlock at the time. (The one at Matlock opened in what had been a doctor's house at the bottom of Steep Turnpike just before I left Ernest Bailey's School in 1945.) I don't remember Mam having the time to read anything but the paper until she was well into her seventies, when she read the romance or mystery novels she borrowed from the mobile library that was introduced just after the war.

Fortunately, despite Mam's fears about my eyesight, both my Aunt Gladys and Grandmother Wallis continued to give me books: collections of stories and poems that I began to learn by heart. Already, at Ambergate School, I had learned the poems every child learned then:

I have a little shadow
That goes in and out with me,
But what can be the use of him
Is more than I can see.

And Tennyson's 'The Brook':
I come from haunts of coot and hern
I make a sudden sally
To sparkle out among the fern
And bicker down the valley.

After I reached puberty, romantic verse such as 'The Highwayman' became favourites.

He'd a French cocked hat on his forehead
A bunch of lace at his chin
A coat of claret velvet
And breeches of brown doeskin.
They fitted with never a wrinkle
His boots were up to the thigh
And he rode with a jewelled twinkle
His pistol butts a-twinkle
His rapier hilt a-twinkle
Under a jewelled sky.

Not your common or garden highwayman. However, over-blown or not, poetry and novels became a larger and larger part of my life, as did girls' school stories. The books my grandmother and aunt gave me for Christmas and birthdays were sometimes what were called *Bumper Books for Girls*, fat tomes containing stories about girls at boarding school. These tales were very popular at the time, although in my class the chance of attending a boarding school of any sort was slim. Nevertheless, I longed to put on a gymslip and have cocoa in the dorm at midnight. How I envied the heroine of *The Worst Girl at St Ethelred's*: kicking over the traces, playing truant, cheeking the Head, shooting the winning goal at hockey. 'Oh, well done, Brenda!' the gym mistress would call in my reverie. 'Jolly good!'

Such was my reading in my early life: poems, schoolgirl's stories, and mysteries, and this didn't change until I was about thirteen when, in the school's library, I discovered Walter Scott.

Today I find his writing a little turgid, but he wrote about the history of Scotland, my favourite country, and I ploughed through every Scott novel I could find.

Not an auspicious beginning to a literary life, perhaps, but at least it was a beginning.

CHAPTER 17
Ninepence to the Shilling

A Derbyshire village (John Grain)

IN OUR SMALL VILLAGE of fewer than five hundred people, I have since counted eleven who were mentally disturbed in some way. This ran the gamut from the severely retarded to the merely eccentric. All were, in local parlance, 'daft' or 'ninepence to the shilling'. (We were not kind to our mentally or physically disadvantaged.)

In addition to the boy who was deemed to be lacking in change, Chadwicknick Lane had two more of these people. One, the grandson of an old lady who lived next door to the Rollinsons, was a young man of twenty or so who wandered about the village, his eyes totally blank. He never worked and never, as far as I know, harmed anyone, but was definitely suffering from some sort of mental disturbance. The other strange person was an old lady named Lizzie who lived a little above us in a house now called Norway. When we moved to Fritchley, she was probably about seventy or so: tall, grey-headed, and with many white bristles about her chin. She was, Mam said, 'a clean old lady', (shades of a Beatle's dad.) She grew gooseberries in her back garden and in the summer had them for sale.

Once, when Beryl was five and I thirteen, Mam sent us up the lane to visit Lizzie and buy a basket of her gooseberries. She presented them to us, already topped and tailed in an old peg basket and covered with a clean white cloth. The berries cost sixpence. We children were never reluctant to go on this errand, because there seemed to be nothing remarkable or frightening about the old woman. She was friendly, even kindly with us, and although a school friend had warned me that she was a witch, I had dismissed the information since the girl had fingered several witches in the community, among them her own grandmother. However, it was true that every full moon Lizzie took her dolly tub, filled it to the brim, and sent the water cascading through her house, sweeping it over the doorstep, down the garden path, and into Chadwicknick Lane. This was no ordinary house cleaning.

Another person who was periodically overcome by the moon lived on the Common, not far from us. The man must have been a trial to his wife because he never worked, although he kept a beautiful garden and grew a lot of vegetables. When there was a full moon, he always stripped off his clothes and ran round our milkman's home field. 'Ay's bin at it again, Mrs Wallis!' Georgie Key would inform Mam when he came the next morning to deliver the milk. 'Ay's bin runnin' rahnd again!' I have read recently that scientists have concluded that the moon has no effect on one's mind, but having seen our two lunatics in action, I'm keeping an open mind.

Further up the Common, in the lane leading to the Quaker guest house, lived another old eccentric who I think of whenever I hear Dylan Thomas's 'A Child's Christmas in Wales'—the part where the young carollers hear 'a thin, dry voice through the keyhole.' Jean Barber once took me and some other children carolling at his house one dark night before Christmas. There was no response to our knocking, not even a thin dry voice; nevertheless, his silence was disconcerting and gave us the same frisson that Thomas's young carollers must have felt. We walked, very quickly, back down the lane. The old man's particular eccentricity was to take a basket of apples from his orchard, stand in the middle of the Common and force drivers to stop, after which he would demand that they buy before he allowed them to drive on.

Down in the village proper, there was Jimmie, who was severely retarded. He lived on the Green, and I remember the local children cat-calling and tormenting the poor child until his mother came out of their cottage to chase them away. There were also two rather simple brothers, Tommy and Billy, who had a farm nearby. They owned, or perhaps rented, a field in Chadwicknick Lane opposite Ballantrae House and would come to it in a cart pulled by their old horse. They were usually asleep, Tommy fat and red-faced, his brother smaller and dark, their heads nodding in unison as the horse found its way to the field gate by itself. Their farm was among the most primitive in the village, and at threshing time (thrashing time in Fritchley speak), when the local farmers gathered at each other's farms to help with that back-breaking task, the threshing meal at their farm was served in a large bowl in the middle of the table, medieval style, the guests plunging their forks into it whenever they felt the urge.

Before our time, an eccentric had lived nearby at The Barn, a large stone house on the corner below Ballantrae. His peculiarity was that he used to lean over his gate when Aunt Flo was passing on the way to her bookkeeping job and say, 'The bright day brings forth the adder'. A clever remark, perhaps, but he said it every time she passed.

Another deranged youth named Smith (no relation to my husband's family) murdered the gloriously beautiful young woman he was 'going with'. Ironically, she and her mother were refugees from the bombing somewhere in the south of the country and had come to Fritchley to escape danger. The girl was a pupil at Herbert Strutt's secondary school in Belper. Everyone in the village was shocked, and no one I spoke to remembered a murder in the village before. Several people assured me that Smith had become violent because he'd 'got a metal plate in his head'. After he killed the girl, the youth committed suicide by hanging himself from a tree in a hillside wood on the Top Hag, close to where I used to take our dog Rabina for a walk. I had been on the hill when the bodies were there and was grateful that I was not the one to find them.

CHAPTER 18

Class: Posh, or Not

IN THE 1930S, ENGLISH society was divided into many layers, each one as thin as sheet mica. My mother didn't consciously set out to teach me the system, but I began to learn it from her and other relatives when I was about five or six. By the time I was twelve, I had discovered that my class depended on any number of subtle qualities: my accent and vocabulary; how I was dressed, and in what kinds of materials; where I lived and in what sort of house; and my family name, if it been around for centuries or was more obscure. The way I pronounced the letter 'a' was also a class marker. A long 'a', as in clahss, ahfter, pahss, we considered posh; a short 'a': class, after, pass, was lower class but acceptable in our milieu, mainly because it wasn't upper class. Ironically, most people in southern England, rich or poor, Cockney or Royal, use the long 'a'.

Money had very little to do with class; a very poor lord was always ahead of a rich farmer in the pecking order. I grew up with this kind of knowledge until it became instinctive for me to 'place' someone within a few moments of meeting him or her. I attempt to subdue it now, but suspect the old instinct still survives to some degree when I meet someone new, especially if they are English.

Perhaps we have Richard Arkwright to thank for the gradual breakdown of the class system after this self-made man came on the scene. Arkwright was born in 1732 into a humble family, his father a yeoman farmer and tailor. Richard had little education, and as a consequence, his English spelling and grammar were faulty throughout his life. Only after he began to experiment successfully with the cotton-spinning machines he helped design did he begin to rise in the world. Eventually he became a very rich man with a title: Sir Richard.

Similar things were happening to men throughout the Derwent Valley and beyond, so that the class system, ever so slightly, must have begun to change as people became confused about class. Here was Arkwright, an extremely rich man with a title, yet one who dropped his aitches like rice at a wedding and had trouble completing a grammatically correct sentence. Even so, the system was still rigid as late as my childhood, and it was the reason I called my mother Mam instead of Mummy; she thought Mummy too upper class.

Class also had to do with many other aspects of life: one's education and if one's parents believed in higher learning for their sons or daughters. Mam didn't believe university, or even grammar school, was necessary for girls; I suspect that she thought it had little to recommend it for anyone at our level in society, and it would not have occurred to her that an education might put a working-class person into a higher social bracket.

I was lucky in that Aunt Flo had been to grammar school, and because of this my father insisted I go to Ernest Bailey's in Matlock when I reached the age of eleven. If he had not, I would not have been allowed to attend school beyond the age of fourteen. Later, when I had the chance of a scholarship to a library school, Mam vetoed it, which probably meant that my father did too. 'We've got the lads to educate', she told me worriedly. Marriage, according to Mam, was the only career open to a woman. A job merely filled the gap between school and the altar, and, unfortunately for me, Dad left most of the parenting to her. I should emphasize that Cis Durward was a loving mother, but also typical of many working-class mothers of the 1930s.

Mam was always very conscious of the class differences between her family and the one she married into. The other Durwards were conscious of it, too. For some reason, as a very young child, and unlike anyone else on either side of my family, I pronounced my name 'Brendah' and my brother's name 'Petah'. Hearing this, Uncle Bud accused his sister of teaching her kids to talk 'swanky'. Jack sometimes teased me, 'I'll bet you'd rather be with your Wallis lot than with us.' This wasn't true. Fortunately, I was at ease in either Matlock with the Durwards, or in Crich or Fritchley with the Wallises; I just chose my vocabulary according to where I was at the moment. This may seem dishonest, but when I was with my Wallis kin, I felt like a Wallis; when with the Durwards, I was a Durward.

Dropping one's aitches was another class indicator. Most children in our part of the country dropped their aitches, and then, if they were talking to someone who spoke correctly, would sometimes become self-conscious and begin putting them back in the wrong places. 'Don't put your h'aitches where there h'are none,' one child would jeer at another, 'H'or you'll come 'urrying 'ome with a h'onion in your h'eye.'

Dialect was also a marker in the class game, and from my Durward relatives, and later my fellow students at the more working-class school at Fritchley, I learned many wonderful local words and phrases. Looking at a list I have compiled, I realize that many of the words were descriptive of people, usually in an unflattering way. For instance: your eyes, if you were unfortunate, could 'stick out like chapel 'at pegs', or you could be 'boss-eyed' (cross-eyed); if you were bandy-legged, you 'couldn't stop a pig in a jennel' (a narrow passage-way), and if your toes turned in, you were 'twilly-toed'. When I was seven or so, I had the misfortune of having one foot that tended to turn in, and Mam and Dad were most concerned about it. We had a postman who turned in both feet and was nicknamed 'Slutherfoot' by the locals; he was pointed out to me as an example of what might happen if I didn't get that foot straightened out.

Other words garnered from the Durwards and my fellow pupils at Fritchley included the word 'mardy', which meant crybaby. To look 'a proper bobby-dazzler' meant that someone admired your outfit—one of our rare complimentary remarks. Then there was rain; we had almost as many words for this as the Inuit are reputed to have for snow. Beginning with the mildest rain, 'dampin' dahn', we then had 'mistin'', closely followed by 'mizzlin'', both of which were said to 'wet you'. It might be thought that all rain does that, but it is true that misting and mizzling, both of which produced a fine haze of moisture that clung to our woollen clothing, seemed to wet us even more than a full downpour. After mizzling rain, we had 'spittin'', when the rain actually formed a few drops that hit the ground here and there. After this, the weather rapidly deteriorated. From 'pourin'' we went quickly to 'lashin'', followed by 'silin'', (siling, an actual word found in the dictionary); followed by 'stair rods', and, finally 'bucketing', or 'coming down 'ole'. All this weather would be presaged by the fact that the sky was 'black o'er Bill's mother's'.

The list of dialect words is long, but a few of the more colourful include: 'fawce', which means craftily clever; 'nesh', meaning you feel the cold unduly, and 'starved' which also means you are cold rather than hungry. If I ate my food too quickly, I was accused of 'gollupping'; if I ate too much, it was called 'gutzin''. A family story has it that an old village lady, on an occasion when numerous family members were visiting and eating inordinately, was heard to grumble, 'Gutzin', gutzin', gutzin', I wish you'd goo wom!' (That is: go home.) Also, if I grumbled I was 'chuntering'; if I made high-pitched, gasping sounds when crying, I was 'chinking', and if I roughhoused I was told to 'stop marlocking about'. Babies that squirmed were described as 'sprottling', and to be hungry was to be 'fair clemmed'. 'Fair' was a word often used to mean 'very'. Also, we often used the phrase 'I'd as leif' do such-and-such, meaning 'I would rather'. (Oddly, I found that phrase in Saul Bellow's *More Die of Heartbreak*.) And finally, mud was 'clarty', a lovely word. Think of peanut butter on the roof of your mouth—that's clarty.

Only after the Second World War, when the troops arrived home and helped vote in a socialist government, did the class situation begin to change substantially. Upper-class English began to disappear as the BBC hired announcers with more middle-class accents; these are now being given their coup de grace by a Cockney-sounding argot. Both speech and feelings of class are much different in England today. After the loosening of class lines during the '50s with the advent of the 'Angry Young Men', in the early twenty-first century, the gap is again widening between the upper class and hoi polloi. As it is across the Atlantic, class today is based largely on money and success—or notoriety.

CHAPTER 19
Settling In

Ballantrae House

AFTER OUR MOVE TO Fritchley, the builders still had to finish tiling the hall, and the developing garden was still being worked over by the man from Heage, the taciturn, elderly man who wore strings round his trousers in order to keep his turn-ups out of the mud. After the gardener left, Dad took over the work with help from Mam when she could find the time. At first, we had only a wire-and-post fence round the garden and the cows browsed right up to it, breathing heavily and tearing at the grass between the buttercups. In Ambergate, everyone had a garden where they grew flowers and vegetables, and it was the same in Fritchley where, in addition to their flower borders and vegetable gardens, many villagers also had an allotment, where the men who had laboured all week in the mines or quarries spent their more relaxed weekends.

I had a garden of my own, as did brother Pete; they were both about ten feet square and were to the side of a concrete path that stretched all the way down the garden, with Mam's washing lines strung between posts at either end. (Her washing routines were the same as at Ambergate, and she still had no washing machine.) My garden was near the final post. There was a lawn near the fence at the back where Dad set up a swing he had bought for us, and nearer to the house was his vegetable garden, where he grew potatoes, peas, beans, broccoli, strawberries, and some gooseberry and blackcurrant bushes. The front of the house had a lawn with a rose tree in the centre and annuals such as lobelia and snapdragons. There was also a rose arch with American pillar roses at the side of the house, where in the spring Dad's bulbs produced drifts of daffodils.

When the garden was fully planted, we again employed the man from Heage, this time to build a sandstone wall round the garden. The stone came from the small private quarry at Ambergrove, where a friend of Dad's quarried and dressed the stone himself. Ballantrae was a happy house, and a refuge whenever I had trouble at school, or later during the war, when things were going badly in France or in the deserts of North Africa, and I feared for my uncles.

We had pets at Ballantrae. Already, at Ambergate, Peter and I had kept rabbits; mine a Dutch one with black on her rear parts, white at the front, and black ears. Pete's was a Belgian Blue, white with a few black spots. I don't remember what we named them. We kept them in a hutch in the garden and fed them mash plus dandelions and dock leaves. The rabbits were not very pettable because they wouldn't hold still, and when we tried to take them up with one hand under their rumps, they scrabbled with their back feet and left welts on our arms. They lasted only a short time after we moved to Ballantrae House. I don't remember which one died of 'podge', which is what we called it when an animal died because we had overfed it. The other was the victim of a fox.

Later, after we had moved to Fritchley and my brother Gilbert was five or six, he was given a puppy, a mongrel that was partly Labrador. We called her Rabina. Mam was not happy when Gib arrived home with this mutt. He had been 'helping' a farmer in Fritchley bring in his hay, and the farmer had seized the opportunity to rid himself of an unwanted pup. Without asking if his parents were willing, he had sent the animal home with Gib. Few mothers can say no when a small child arrives home cradling a puppy; however, Mam soon made it clear that Rabina was not to be a house dog, so Dad bought a kennel for her, and she spent most of her life out in the hen field. Poor Rabina would have loved to live in the house, and her howls when she wanted to come inside could have wrung the heart of a zombie. She was totally untrained because no one in the family thought to train her, or even knew how; consequently, when allowed off her leash, she bounded about as if on springs and zipped through the countryside like a horizontal streak of black lightning. One day Gib found her shot dead under the hedge in a nearby field. We suspected that a local farmer had killed her, a whey-faced, rather evil-looking young man who had a farm nearby. Quite possibly Rabina had been playing havoc with his cows. I'm not sure how everyone reacted. My parents were probably relieved because Rab had been a difficult mutt, largely through our own fault; Gib, no doubt was desolate, and Pete, Beryl, and I were at least saddened. However it was, the family didn't own another dog until Bruce, Beryl's Scottie, came on the scene after I had left home. Bruce was a house dog, a trained one.

When he was older, Gib kept ferrets in a small hutch in the garden. He and his friends used them when they went hunting rabbits in the nearby woods. He also had a gun, a .22, which he kept in a locked case in his bedroom. Uncle Gib in Scotland had trained him well in procedures to follow when owning a firearm.

The family lived in Ballantrae House from 1937 until the 1960s. In 1951, I married and left for America, and then Pete, Beryl, and finally Gib married and left home, too, and my parents were rattling about in a house much too big for them. In addition, my father was ill, so it was time to move. They bought a bungalow on the Top Lane in Crich Carr; they named it Colmonell in memory of our Scottish holidays.

Gib: The Young Hunter

CHAPTER 20
The Village Postman

Fritchley Post Office

VILLAGES, THEN AND NOW, have their characters; Fritchley had several, but borrowed its most colourful one from Ambergate. When we had lived in the valley, we had been used to seeing postman Jackie pedalling his sit-up-and-beg bicycle through the village, his one arm clutching the handlebars, and what was left of his other one clamping the strap of his mailbag to his side. Jackie had lost an arm, depending upon whose story you believed, either in Flanders Fields or in a barny outside a pub. He liked his beer, but I suspect the war was the real reason for his loss. Many of the wounded were given jobs in the post office after the First World War, but it was only after we moved that we discovered Jack's bailiwick was Fritchley.

Jackie was a red-faced, brawny man. Each day he cycled from his home in Ambergate, two miles along the Amber River valley to the bottom of Bullbridge Hill, dressed in his postman's uniform with its flat, peaked hat and with his large leather bag slung over one shoulder. At the bottom of the hill, Jackie was forced to dismount and wheel his bike, one-handed, up the mile or so of the very steep road that led to Fritchley. There, he visited the post office, collected the mail that had been delivered earlier by van, and, leaving his bike behind, set off on foot for his first delivery of the day. There were two deliveries then, and they involved a great deal of walking both uphill and down. The village is long, stretching two miles to the northwest as far as the Tors, and southeast downhill to Fritchley Brook and beyond. The village was also about a mile and a half wide, so that by the time Jackie returned to the post office, he had walked several miles and was ready for lunch and a breather before it was time to collect his second batch of letters and start out again.

Jackie was not a quiet man. We often heard him coming a while before he put in an actual appearance. 'Orders for you, Jack, me old lad! Orders!' he would yell before he even rounded the corner of the lane that ran past our house. He knew my father was a commercial traveller, and each day he delivered several business letters. When Jackie arrived at our door, he always slammed the knocker up and down, still yelling that he was bringing orders. Christmas was Jackie's noisiest time. On Christmas Eve, many of the households he visited gave him a Christmas 'box': a tip acknowledging his work for us during the year. My mother always had an envelope waiting for him and an invitation to come in for a small tot of rum and one of her mince pies. Unfortunately, quite a few of Jackie's customers did the same, with the result that, one Christmas Eve, he was found sleeping blissfully under a hedge, his head cradled on his letter sack.

The postman was not too proud to read our postcards and then go yodelling about the village spreading the news that, say, the Barritt family was spending a weekend at Blackpool, or that the Jones baby had arrived. During the war he could often be heard carolling, 'He's coming home, me old love! Better get the bed warmed!', and a young wife would come running, pink-faced, to her gate to collect the card that told her that her husband had leave and was on his way home. Other days, when Jackie was unnaturally quiet, we held our breath until he had passed our gate, fearing that he was carrying a letter from the War Office telling of some relative's wounding, or his death.

Jackie seldom made a mistake, but one day when I was seventeen, he presented me with a missive from a local lying-in hospital, telling me that space would be held for me when my time came. We had two prisoner-of-war camps in the vicinity, one for Germans and one for Italians. Strict discipline was used with the Germans, who were usually kept behind barbed wire with sentry posts at the corners of their prison compound. But the Italians were treated much more leniently. As soldiers we found them rather a joke; their hearts didn't seem to be in the fight, and in North Africa they had sensibly surrendered in droves. As prisoners, many of them worked for local farmers and could often be seen walking, unescorted, about the countryside. A girl with a similar name to mine became over friendly with one of these prisoners and had got herself 'in trouble', as it was phrased. The letter was hers. We gave it back to Jackie to re-deliver, and thereafter heard him laughing like a drain on his way back down the village.

One day when I was home from America, visiting my sister who lives in Ambergate, I met Jackie near his home. I was about forty-five at the time and had not seen him since I was eighteen. He hadn't changed a bit.

'Hello, Jack,' I said. 'I bet you don't remember me. I'm Brenda Wallis from Fritchley.'

Jackie looked at me for a while, until finally light dawned, and his jaw sagged.

'Eeh, I say!' He shook his head sadly. 'You 'ave altered!'

CHAPTER 21
Becoming a Primitive Methodist

The Primitive Methodist Chapel, Fritchley

WHEN, AFTER DR ANDERSON'S urging we moved up into the hills, I became a Primitive Methodist. Had I not become a Methodist, or a Congregationalist, a member of the Church of England, or even a Quaker, the children at school would have ostracized me further.

Fritchley was a very religious village in the 1930s; not only did most children attend one Sunday school or another, but many of their mothers went to the adult services too. Their fathers were a different story. Most of the men were involved in hard, manual labour and Sunday being their only day of rest, they left it to their families to keep them well in with the Creator; nevertheless, all the religions in the village had substantial congregations. There was a Quaker Meeting House near the post office, and although I was not aware of any little Quakers in the school, Fritchley was a thriving Quaker village at the time and well known in parts of Pennsylvania where some of the Friends had emigrated. A Quaker family named Ludlow welcomed non-drinking, clean-living vegetarians to their guesthouse on the Common, where visitors spent warm summer evenings country dancing on the lawn. The visitors also liked to hike and bird-watch, and tended to pat us little villagers on the head and give us sweets. They were probably unaware that we had christened them 'Ludlow's Loonies'.

It was Jean Barber—she who escorted me to school—who insisted I become a Methodist, because that was what she and her sisters and brother were. I was not unwilling; I would be able to continue my conversations with God that had begun after my enlightenment at Ambergate School. Mam, that scoffer, raised no objection, although her look was ironic at times. After all, she was doing her own conforming to village mores by joining the Women's Institute, so perhaps she realized that I, too, was undergoing the same kinds of social pressure. I had no idea then of the differences among the various denominations or I might have chosen to attend the Church of England housed in our school building, but Jean was Methodist and, willy-nilly, that's what I became. The Fritchley Primitive Methodists were quite strict, which meant the Rollinson children were not allowed to play games on Sundays. Mam got me into hot water with Jean soon after we moved to Fritchley when she had the temerity to wash my baby sister's napkins on the Sabbath and hang them out to dry in the garden.

The Primitive Methodist Chapel, now a private house, still stands in Sun Lane opposite what was the school and C of E church. (The school, too, is now a house.) The chapel had one whitewashed room and church-like windows with plain glass. In this cold box of a place, we sat and listened to Bible stories from an old lady named Miss Leaf, who lived in a cottage further down the village. I don't remember the hymns, although there must have been some, because every year we had to rehearse for Our Sermons ('ah sairmons', to use a local pronunciation).

Our Sermons was an annual event in the spring when, on different Sundays, each of the chapels held ceremonies to which members of the other chapel and the church were invited. The ceremony had two parts: in the morning we children and the adults would set off for the chapel to meet with the musician—in our case a violinist—and after we were gathered, we went about the village rather in the manner of carollers, singing hymns on the Green, outside each place of worship, and at the ends of Allen and Fritchley Lanes. In the afternoon, after we had been home for dinner, we girls would put on our best frocks and the boys their best jackets and short pants, in most cases all bought especially for the occasion. My first year in Fritchley I made a terrible social gaffe: I wore my new dress for the morning's stroll about the village instead of saving it for the afternoon, thus earning another rebuke from Jean.

After the morning's hymn singing round the village, followed by the midday meal, we returned to the chapel for the actual sermons. For this event, we would find that banks of seats had been placed in steps on either side of the chapel and that the various congregations were filing into them. A visiting preacher gave the sermon, after which everyone joined in the hymn-singing. Jean Barber often sang a solo, usually one of the then popular 'one-word' songs such as 'Trees' or 'Because', neither of them very church-like ditties.

Because the school was Church of England the school authorities presented me with a Bible, and one of the other children taught me how to use it to 'find out what God wants'. If I didn't know how to handle some situation, such as whether to confess to Mam that I, and not Pete, had taken that threepenny bit from her purse, I was to close my eyes, open the Bible at random, run a finger down the page, and read the chosen verse. I did this quite often, until one day it dawned on me that the advice given never actually covered the problem involved.

My religious fervour continued until I began to meet children, not only of other Christian denominations, but of other religions entirely. There seemed to be a veritable lucky dip of them, and every one of them assumed theirs was the way. It seemed to me that you put your hand into the barrel and brought out whatever your religion was to be, and this depended to a large degree on your family background and whether any Jean Barbers were in the vicinity. That was when, as I looked at the plethora of religions about the world, it occurred to me that they couldn't all be right. In fact, maybe none of them was, and there was another 'truth' we hadn't yet been smart enough to determine.

CHAPTER 22

Accepted at Last!

I WAS ONLY NINE when we moved to Fritchley, and because the local girls were unfriendly, for a while I felt lost. I no longer had a best friend living anywhere near, no one like Margaret with whom to roam about the countryside gathering bouquets of dog daisies for our mothers, no one with whom to play cricket or run about after hoops or conspire to tease our friend Rita.

After school, I played ball by myself, bouncing it against the side of the house and chanting some ritual or other, and now and then I would walk down the Hag to Ambergate to visit Margaret, or she would walk up to Fritchley so that we could play together as always. But it was not the same. During those years I spent a lot of time working in my garden, or taking Sunday walks with Dad, or visiting my grandparents. The only game I remember playing with the village children after school was one they called "Oller, 'oller', in which someone designated to be 'it' would take off through the village and beyond. He (it was usually a he) would be required to 'holler' every so often so that we could hunt him down. If he failed to do so, we yelled in unison, "Oller! 'Oller! If you don't shout, we shan't foller!' All ages of children played this game, haring about the village and the nearby fields and woods. I don't remember that we ever caught our prey, even after we had heard him hollering.

The Tors, Crich

I also began to take solitary walks, either down the Top Hag or else up Chadwicknick Lane to the Tors. There I could wander for a quarter of a mile or more, along an edge of local gritstone that overlooked the neighbouring village of Crich. The views were spectacular, especially to the west, where the River Derwent made its way down the valley with its comforting grassy or wooded hills on either side. To the east, I could look over the village of Crich to Culland Wood near Barn Close Farm where Joe and little Tom Smith lived, and beyond it to where Ripley's pithead gear punctuated the skyline. To the north was also a view of Crich village with its church and the Stand.

Another amusement was the local cinema, again brought to my attention by Jean Barber who revealed to me the joys of 'the pictures' on a Saturday morning. In Crich, just beyond the King's Arms pub where Dad was a 'regular', there is a long, red-brick building—now a house—that was then the local cinema. This we called Crich Haybarn, a palace of delight where, every Saturday morning, children spent their tuppences for a seat at the front, and courting couples of fourteen or fifteen would splurge sixpence for luxurious double seats at the back.

Once settled in our seats, we would enter the world of sepia-coloured films. I have not seen films in brown and white since, but that was the colour of many of the epics that were shown at Crich Haybarn. They were serial films, usually about cowboys and Indians, and in my memory the episodes often ended just as the maiden was about to be either ravished or saved by the Indian villain (or hero), or the herd of buffalo was about to hurtle over the cliff. We were supposed to come again the following week to find out what happened to the heroine (or buffalo herd), but I found that I seldom did. Jean would forget to invite me, or she was too busy to go, or I'd lost interest. I was not allowed to go alone until I was older, when the films were the Three Stooges, Charlie Chaplin, or George Formby.

In addition to Hollywood entertainment, we also produced our own concerts. The local Women's Institute once put on a 'minstrel' show in blackface—shamefully, I think now, although I didn't think so at the time. (Then, most people were thought-lessly racist. In most small villages, people had never met a black person because there were none; moreover, our attitude towards Africans was skewed by colonialism. I saw my first person of colour during the war when American servicemen were stationed near Derby.)

One year, our teachers organized us in order to give a concert at the Methodist Chapel, which had a stage in a room big enough to accommodate a large audience. Jean Barber and a boy of thirteen who, to his chagrin, still had a beautiful soprano voice, were scheduled to sing; another boy did card tricks taught to him by his father, which on the night of the show turned out to be impossible to see from the pews at the back of the chapel. There were also a couple of jugglers, one or two home-written skits, lots of choral singing, and a young comedian whose jokes had to be closely monitored by his teacher before the show. One or two classmates and I were ordered to learn a poem and then recite it, complete with suitable gestures. My verse was titled 'The Squirrel'; I've forgotten who wrote it. Because I was shy, the idea of standing up in full view of an audience filled me with terror. After all, my mother would be in the audience with her great expectations, as would my mother's sister Gladys, plus Aunt Flo and my Wallis grandmother, not to mention numerous neighbours, and a passel of older boys who could be relied upon to jeer and make loud and probably vulgar comments.

As the evening for the show approached, I became more and more agitated, especially since Mam and my other relatives seemed thrilled by the idea that 'our Brennie' was to perform. About a week before my appearance, Mam took me to Matlock, where at Marsden's emporium (now an antique shop by the river bridge), she bought for me a suitable reddish-bronze jersey dress and jacket. (English squirrels were red in those days—since then, imported grey ones have taken over much of their territory.) On the evening of the show, I waited, dry-mouthed and trembling, for my ordeal. It came and, knees knocking, I crept out onto the stage where an ocean of white, expectant faces awaited me. I stroked my imaginary tail, I recited, and when I was finished, the audience applauded (loudly, I was gratified to note). It was over! After taking a bow, I strutted off the stage. I wouldn't have minded being asked to do an encore.

CHAPTER 23

School Holidays

OUR SUMMER HOLIDAYS STRETCHED from the beginning of August until the first week of September and seemed gloriously endless. It was then that I enjoyed visits of a fortnight or so at Derwent Villas, my Wallis grandparents' home beside the canal in Whatstandwell. Granddad was usually busy in his study upstairs, noisily typing his daily column on his old-fashioned typewriter and puffing out clouds of smoke from his pipe. I would spend the mornings 'helping' Granny with a little dusting or weeding, but more often than not in fascinated perusal of *Woman's Own*, a magazine of my Aunt Flo's that always contained a love story. These narratives were innocent and more or less the same each week, the protagonists wearing the same kinds of clothing: the men in either evening dress or a tweed jacket and flannel bags; the women with marcelled hair and adorned in long backless frocks, or in woollen skirts and jumpers with pearls, depending on the story's milieu.

I also learned many 'beauty secrets' from the magazines, such as how to whiten my elbows by cupping them in lemon halves, or how to tighten my eleven-year-old pores by rubbing my face with slices of cucumber. To me this was a fascinating new world, and secretly, when Aunt Flo was at work, I would try on her make-up, which she kept in a piano stool in the attic bedroom I shared with her. My grandmother didn't seem to notice my bedizened look.

There was also the Letters to the Editor column in the magazine, which I later learned to call the 'Done Wrongs', because the desperate young women correspondents would confess to 'Auntie Mabs', the letters editor, that they had been out with a young man and had 'done wrong'. These letters mystified me; had these young women allowed themselves to be *kissed*? Nor was I much enlightened by the replies, which were of the 'go thou and sin no more' variety.

Granny Wallis and Brenda on our walk to Cromford and Wirksworth

Granny Wallis and Flo were avid walkers, which meant that when I went to stay with them, I was a walker too. Theirs were not trivial strolls. One in particular took us along the canal towpath to Cromford with a stop for lunch at a little café ´ in the marketplace.

Afterwards, we continued on up the hill towards Wirksworth and Bole Hill, down Longway Bank, past the entrance to Birchwood Farm, and so home to Derwent Villas in time for tea. The walk was easily ten miles long, and Granny was over sixty. On shorter expeditions, Granny and I sometimes hiked up the very steep hill from her house to the Top Lane and took Bryan's Steps through the fields to Crich. There, Granny would have an errand, perhaps at the cobbler's shop just below the Cross, or at the village stores in the marketplace. Granddad was never included in these expeditions. He took his walks very early in the morning, and spent the rest of the day either reading or writing in his study, the front bedroom at Derwent Villas.

In the evenings, we played games. Tiddlywinks was a favourite, the thick plush of the best tablecloth ideal because it made the counters hop into the eggcup in a satisfactory manner. The more counters that landed in the cup, the more points you won. Granddad was good at this and a most enthusiastic and noisy player; Granny would go into fits of giggles at his antics.

Granny and Granddad had a similar sense of humour. Granddad loved to tell the story of how Granny, busy weeding, was greeted by a male acquaintance walking down the path that ran parallel to her garden. They spoke for a while of gardening and plants, and then Granny offered, 'Would you like some lavender to put in your drawers, Mr So-and-so?' Granddad thought this hilarious. He was also amused when someone, talking to Granny when she was an old lady, remarked of a neighbour, 'He's a bit of an old woman, Mrs Wallis.' These mild jokes would amuse them both and became part of family lore. Grandmother also had her stories. One was of a young woman, a friend of her youth, who went to a dance wearing the latest in her collection of (paste) jewellery. Nobody noticed, and after a while, she felt compelled to burst out with, 'Oh, I do feel hot in my new ring!'

When I stayed with my Durward relatives in Matlock, the routine was different, as was the reading material. This consisted of *The News of the World*, a tabloid rather racy for its time, in which the news was largely concerned with something called carnal knowledge. I found this just as mysterious as the Done Wrongs.

Walking was not a top priority with Granny Durward; she had plenty of exercise cleaning the bank and looking after her own house, and since she had begun her working life washing dishes at a hydro at the age of eleven, walking just for the heck of it was not on her agenda. Instead, neighbours along the row often visited us, or we visited them, Jack and I sitting quietly so that no one would notice us as we listened to the local gossip. One neighbour, whom Jack and I called 'Horsey' Ballington because of her long face and lugubrious expression, usually had us stifling our giggles in our lair behind the sofa, especially when her gossip swerved towards the doings of a young woman Jack had christened the Blonde Bomber. (Jack gave several people nicknames, among them his own mother whom he called 'Sizme'.) Horsey regaled her audience with stories of the Blonde Bomber's exploits among the wounded airmen who had been sent to Rockside Hydro to recuperate. The Bomber's husband was meanwhile fighting somewhere overseas. Granny Durward was shocked: 'Eeh, I say!' she invariably exclaimed on hearing these titbits, her eyes wide.

Uncles also visited 2, St John's Terrace with their wives or girlfriends, all to be greeted by Granny's 'Eeh, I say!' as they approached through the passage from the front door. When Uncle George was courting his Brenda and announced plans to go for a walk, Granny would say, 'I bet our Bren would like a walk with you, our George.' She was, of course, sending me to act as a 'gooseberry', but George was quite amiable about it. Usually, the three of us strolled as far as the Wishing Stone, a large rock in a small park about a half-mile away. After we had visited its small gazebo, and I had pretended not to notice Uncle George's brief disappearance behind a hedge with his girlfriend, we would then stroll back.

Very occasionally, I took a walk with one or more of the uncles, usually with a goal in view: a collection of sticks for the fire, or to the shops for bottles of ginger beer (sold in stone jars with marbles in their necks to help stop the bubbles from escaping). Or Jack and I were sent to fetch the usual 'two pennorth of balm', that is, yeast, from a shop on Smedley Street so that Granny could bake. Uncles Bernard and Reg often took me on walks over the fields to Riber Castle. I especially remember another walk, on Matlock moor in 1938, because a murderer named Smedley was at large at the time, and the uncles spoke about what they would do if they came across him. Smedley was a young man from a prominent Matlock family, possibly the one that had produced some of the Matlock hydros in the nineteenth century. He had murdered his girlfriend in a fit of rage. The victim had 'been lead-ing him on', according to Gladys, meaning that she had teased him sexually. In those unenlightened times, this was often the excuse put forward for a woman being attacked, as though this exoner-ated the offending male. The murder took place at a house on the hill immediately above my grandmother's home. The guilty man was later found hiding in some farm buildings on what was to become my father-in-law's Birchwood Farm; he had been sleep-ing in the barn and eating turnips out of the field. After serving a long sentence, he was released from prison in the late nineties.

CHAPTER 24

The War Begins

'**ME DAD SAYS AS** there'll be a war,' a child at school told me, her eyes round as a marmoset's, 'safe as 'ouses!'

'Houses won't be all that safe if there is a war,' Granddad Wallis told me grimly when I reported this. He had lived through the Great War with its trench warfare, zeppelins, and four-winged planes and knew to expect worse next time.

As war approached, my parents listened to the BBC news more frequently than before. Dad had been in the Royal Navy during the Great War, and even though he had seen no action, like my grandfather, he was apprehensive. Millions had been slaughtered in the conflict that had ended only eighteen years before, leaving the country traumatized. Dad was only thirty-nine when the Second World War was declared, but fortunately his job was officially declared a 'reserved occupation' because he kept vital supplies moving from his company to the arms factories in Sheffield, Derby, Leicester, and other nearby towns. The adults were obviously worried, and their uneasiness transferred itself to us children. At playtime we regaled each other with tales about the perfidy of Germans and about the trenches and casualties in the previous war.

Then came Munich and the spurious 'peace in our time'; we thought we were off the hook. How everyone cheered Neville Chamberlain, the man with the umbrella, waving his piece of white paper from the steps of his plane as he returned with a peace agreement with Hitler. 'Toodle umber umber, toodle umber umber/Toodle aye ay/Any umberellas, any umberellas to mend today?' was our song at playtime for a while. Shamefully, we had given away a huge chunk of Czechoslovakia to the Nazis, but even that wasn't going to save us. On September 3, 1939, my Wallis grandparents, Dad, and I gathered round the Pye wireless in the sitting room at Derwent Villas and heard Chamberlain announce that we were at war. We had a non-aggression pact with Poland, an agreement that if either country were attacked, the other would enter the war in support. On September 1, Hitler had inflicted his blitzkrieg on Poland.

'They'll have to bring Churchill in now', Dad said.

His mother looked anxious. 'Oh, Jack! But he's not a gentleman!'

Churchill, of course, belonged to a powerful family; what Granny meant by 'a gentleman' was a soft-spoken and ultimately unwarlike person, in other words, Chamberlain. Father snorted that that 'old fool' would be useless.

Before then, the outside world had tended to break in only on royal occasions. One such memory took place in 1934 on a day of thick fog. I was playing in my bedroom when Mam entered and stood looking dejectedly out of my window. 'It's Princess Marina's wedding day,' she announced dolefully, 'and just look at the weather!' I had no idea who the bride was or why Mam cared, or even if London was also blanketed in fog, but it turned out that Marina was a Greek princess who was marrying the Duke of Kent, a son of George V. The princess seems to have been popular, because for a while after her wedding, there was a craze for 'Princess Marina' hats. Even then, people were beginning to become obsessed with celebrities, perhaps as a result of the more widespread reporting of news by radio.

Another royal occasion was in 1935, the King's Jubilee year, when Mam took me to join the neighbours and their children to stand excitedly in an arc in front of the Hurt Arms. We waited for what seemed like hours until, at last, a long black limousine glided towards us down the Belper Road and slowed a little as it passed before continuing east towards Ripley. I couldn't see the King at all but caught a glimpse of Queen Mary and her toque; she waved graciously. The occasion was over. What impresses me now is that I remember no motorcycle escort, or other cars, although they must surely have been there. Some years later, my parents began to talk, dismissively, it seemed to me, about the late king's son, Edward, who had abdicated from his position merely because 'he wanted that American'. This was followed shortly thereafter by the coronation of George VI, which we heard about on the wireless. All these happenings were part of a more innocent world.

The earliest glimpses I had of the wider world, even before the war, was hearing that there was some sort of trouble in Spain, and something called the 'Rape of Nanking' in China. I saw photographs of the Japanese destruction of that city and remember it because I'd overheard my father and grandparents discussing how even children had been massacred. My parents also discussed Kristallnacht and the rise of the Nazis, my father muttering about someone he called 'that hound, Hitler'. After this, there was much talk among the grownups about possible war, and I could see that my parents were becoming worried. My father had been in the Navy during the Great War, and although his experiences had been comparatively mild, like others of his generation, he remembered the huge number of casualties, and what older friends had told him about the horrors of trench warfare.

The first year of the war was labelled the 'Phony War', because at first, as far as we were concerned, very little happened. In the east, the German army devastated Poland and herded its Jewish population into ghettos, but in the west, after initial naval attacks in the Orkneys, they sat in their bunkers on the Siegfried Line trying to outstare the French who were defending their Maginot Line nearby. Defiantly, we children sang, 'We're goin'a hang out the washing on the Siegfried Line/Have you any dirty washing, mother dear?'

At school there was much posturing: we made jokes about Hitler and his moustache and sang a song about the Italian fascist dictator, Mussolini, based on the song 'Roll Along Covered Wagon, Roll Along'. Another song of the period was 'Run, Rabbit, Run'.

Almost as soon as war was declared, the government issued us with ration books and identity cards and had us register with a butcher or grocer so that we could buy only from those particular shops. Butter, sugar, cheese, milk, meat, fruits and vegetables, clothing, petrol and coal were either 'on ration' or else were soon extremely scarce. Eventually our individual rations were reduced to one egg a week, two ounces of butter, a quarter pound of tea, one ounce of cheese, and two of bacon. We were allowed only a few ounces of lard, a move beneficial to our health, since our mothers invariably used it to make pastry, which was delicious but bad for us. In those innocent days, we had not yet heard of cholesterol.

There was also a 'points' system for tinned foods, although these became unobtainable as the Battle of the Atlantic got under way and supply ships were sunk. Hard-pressed shopkeepers began to ask sardonically of housewives, 'Don't you know there's a war on?' This was after the women had spent an hour or more queuing for some scarce item only to find it was sold out by the time they had advanced to the counter.

Milk, too, was rationed. Our milkman, Georgie Key, carried it to us from his cart in a large can, and using a half-pint dipper, measured out our ration into Mam's jugs. Later, milkmen left the milk on our doorsteps in bottles with cardboard caps. Later still, the caps were made of tinfoil with such shine that it attracted the tomtits, which learned to peck the lids from the bottles so they could drink the cream. Milk was not homogenized then, and the cream rose to the top.

Rationing happened over time, not all at once, but by the end of 1940, everything was in short supply, especially goods that came from abroad. Bananas and oranges were soon as rare as gold and were not seen again until after the war. We Britons were now dependent on what we could grow ourselves, although even before the war Britain had not been self-sufficient in food. Now ships were commandeered to bring in armaments and petrol for tanks and aeroplanes, and as time went on food became even more scarce.

Of course, what we children missed most were toffees. After our move to Fritchley, Gladys had gone to work part-time in a sweetshop at nearby Ambergrove, and at the beginning of the war sometimes brought us a few extra sweets. But eventually there were no sweets of any kind to be had, and the shop closed; sugar and sweets were rationed until 1953, other commodities until 1954. The shortage of sugars and fats was good for our overall health—no one was obese—but we children sadly missed our cakes and sweets.

During the war, and afterwards, we were still short of food, particularly towards the end of a ration period. We children were sometimes given a baked potato and a tiny slice of cheese for mid-day dinner, while my mother and Gladys had only an Oxo cube dissolved in hot water.

Matches were also in short supply, and one of my jobs was to create 'spills' out of folded paper. We kept these wands, about ten inches long, in an empty jam jar near the fireplace, so that when anyone wanted to light another fire (a rare occurrence) the gas stove, or a cigarette, they ignited the spill at the fire and applied it to the gas stove or the cigarette before extinguishing it and putting it back in the jar.

Once war was declared, we British children became very proud of our overseas possessions. The Empire was, our teachers told us, a sort of benevolent society in which we 'brought light into darkest Africa' and such places—took up 'the white man's burden', in other words. (Yes, I know, I know!) Wartime made us hyper-patriotic, and we celebrated Empire Day on May 24 with increased fervour, proudly displaying our Empire Medals: round brass medallions with a lion and the words 'British Empire Union' on one side, and on the other the figure of a woman and the words 'For God, King and Empire' which we hung round our necks on their red, white, and blue ribbons. The teachers also lectured us about the Empire and pointed out all the red bits on the map. The Empire, they assured us, was that part of the world on which the sun never sets. Sixty years later the sun has, indeed, gone down. (Now, across the Atlantic, there is vainglorious boasting about being the 'Leader of the Free World'. That notion too is turning sour; no one ever learns from history.)

At the beginning of the war, Mam and Gladys continued to bake bread for the family; however, with the coming of hostilities, millers started to refine their flour less vigorously than before and to leave in wheat germ and bran so that the flour was brown—and more nutritious. Mam, quite sure that 'rubbish' had been left in the flour and, determined that her family should continue to enjoy her superior white bread, spent hours, with Gladys's help, sieving the bran and wheat germ from the flour through a piece of muslin held over the bread pancheon—a large, earthenware bowl used in mixing bread dough. On baking days, I was sent down to Barratt's shop just above the school for our usual 'two pennorth of balm'. I loved yeast and had often nibbled away quite a lot of it before I got back to the house. Yeast was not granulated then but came in a square block and had the consistency of soft cheese.

During the war, farming was a reserved occupation, which meant that farmers were not eligible for call-up because they were needed to help keep us, and a growing number of foreigners (Free French and Free Poles, not to mention thousands of German and Italian prisoners of war), in food. Householders were encouraged to join in and 'dig for victory'. We already had an extensive vegetable garden, but now Dad planted broccoli among the roses and grew extra of everything. Enthusiastically, I flattened my rock garden and planted lettuce, which turned out to grow very badly there, despite the fact that my garden was well shaded. We produced so many potatoes that Dad had to make a 'clamp', a sort of cave in the soil, where he stored the surplus potatoes over the winter.

Shortly after war began, having decided that we should keep hens to help augment our food supply, Dad bought a flock of twelve Rhode Island Reds and housed them in a shed in the field. For a while we were able to buy food for them, but we also saved our vegetable peelings and boiled this 'mash' in a bucket on the kitchen stove. The hens were free-range, and because they also picked up quite a lot of nourishment from the field, they kept us well supplied with eggs. Occasionally, one of them went 'broody', meaning her egg supply dried up, and when this happened Dad bought a clutch of fertile eggs from a local farmer and shut the broody in a small cage with the eggs beneath her nested in a pile of hay. After the chicks hatched, the hen began to lay her own eggs again. These were the lucky broodies; unlucky ones that didn't return to laying were destined for the pot. Free-range hens often 'lay away', that is, laid their eggs anywhere but in their nests, so that we children were often sent to search the edges of the field and beneath the bushes, looking for them.

At Christmas there was usually a shortage of birds for the table, and one year Mam decided that Dad would have to wring the neck of one of our hens. Dad loved his food, but he hated this job with a passion. He was never very good at it, and often the indignant fowl would escape his murderous clutches and flee to safety across the field. Once, in desperation, he took a hatchet, laid the unfortunate bird with its neck across a log, and severed its head with one blow. The hen had the last word, however, and Dad watched in horror as its headless torso ran wildly about the field. 'It almost cackled,' he told us.

Even though miners were not subject to call-up, there was a shortage of coal for domestic use, since a great deal of it was needed in the smelting of metals for use in the armament factories. As a result, our coal ration was small, which meant that we often had only one fire going in the house, the one that heated the oven and the hot water for the bathroom. This left the sitting room and bedrooms icy. English houses had no central heating in those days, and in winter going to bed could be an ordeal. Before the war, we sometimes had a fire in our bedrooms at night if we were ill, and hot water bottles, which we filled with scalding-hot water. My grannies had no such refinements, and when I went to stay with Granny Wallis, she would heat a brick for me in her side oven, wrap it in an old vest, and present it to me to 'take the chill off' the bed. The same was true in Matlock, and even when clutching my brick, I would have to keep my knees to my chest because it was too cold to stretch my legs to the bottom of the bed. On many occasions I could see my breath in the bedroom; once the contents of the chamber pot froze. Most people had a chamber pot under their bed—'guzzunders' we children called them, that is, the vessel that guzzunder the bed. After the war started, we called them Jerries, our slang term for Germans. Even in houses like ours, where the lavatory was not across the yard, one lost less heat crouching over a chamber pot than scuttling along an icy landing to the bathroom.

Of course, with wartime rationing a brisk black market developed. Mam suspected local butchers of killing more animals than they had licenses to do so. 'Them butchers live off the fat of the land!' she would huff. Sometimes, it would be possible, if you knew the right people in a shop, to sneak home with a little extra. Those who never ate meat were allowed an ounce or so extra of cheese a week, and many families suddenly discovered that they had a previously unsuspected vegetarian in their midst.

Petrol was rationed, and although Dad was allowed extra because of his work, his territory was large, and it was never enough. Again, this was solved by recourse to the black market. Dad's friend, who ran a garage, kept the car's tank filled for him whenever he had a little petrol to spare. When I finally realized what was happening, I was both ashamed and afraid. Ashamed because I knew that oil tankers were being torpedoed out in the Atlantic and pictured the drowning sailors screaming amid the flames, and afraid because someone might find out, and we would be disgraced. I think now that most people had to resort to some form of skullduggery during the war in order to survive. Dad at least had the excuse that his work contributed to the war effort.

For a brief time during the war, some drivers bought a cloth-covered, balloon-like object, which they attached to the roof of their car and filled with a gas that was supposed to power it. It was soon discovered to be a very inefficient, not to say dangerous, method of locomotion, and after a while we saw no more of them.

Clothing was also rationed, and for this we were issued 'points', small coupons that had to be accumulated until we had enough for, say, a pair of shoes or a new coat. Items demanded more or fewer points depending on how much material was used in the garment. To save material, turn-ups on men's trousers were banned for the duration, although at the same time, children were given extra clothing coupons because they outgrew their clothes. Needless to say, we were encouraged to 'make do and mend', and by the end of the war, our clothes were threadbare and shabby in the extreme. At any one time throughout my grammar school career, I had one gymslip, two blouses, one skirt for weekends, one gabardine Mac, a couple of vests, a liberty bodice, four much-mended pairs of lisle stockings, and eight pairs of knickers. Because leather was scarce, our shoes often had wooden soles so that we accused each other of clattering about like Dutchmen. We were constantly growing out of our clothes, particularly our shoes, and heaven help the last child in a family, because he or she almost never had anything new. It was a happy day for the women when a German airman bailed out anywhere in the vicinity, and his parachute silk appeared for sale in the local market.

At the time, most women wore headscarves in the winter, squares of material that they folded into a triangle and knotted under their chins, peasant fashion. In winter, children wore pixie hats: an oblong of knitting folded over, the long sides stitched together and ribbons attached to the two open ends to be tied under the chin.

In addition to rationing, there was the blackout when it was mandated that all windows had to be curtained in thick, black material so that no chink of light would alert the German bombers to the presence of towns and cities. Streetlights were turned off, and the lights of cars, and even the torches we used to find our way in the dark had their own circle of blackout cardboard with a small slit in it. Torches were never to be pointed towards the sky, and we used them sparingly because their batteries were hard to find. Air raid wardens were employed in every community to go round and see to it that no one was showing any light; they came knocking at our door several times.

At the beginning of the war, Mam not only blacked out the windows but covered all the panes with a flour paste to which she fixed old lace curtains. This was to stop flying glass in case we were bombed. In the first years of the war, we children moved downstairs to sleep. Pete's bed and mine were brought down into the dining area, while Gladys and Beryl slept in the sitting room. Mam and Dad stayed upstairs, their bedroom doubling as a dining room. Gladys found that carrying our dinners up and down the stairs was so inconvenient that we were once again sleeping upstairs by the second year of the war.

Signposts were also removed. The theory was that any invading Germans would oblige us by becoming lost. There was a finger post at the end of the bottom Hag that pointed variously to Crich, Fritchley, and Bullbridge, each less than a mile apart. This, too, was removed, although it was suggested by some wag that it be turned round so that the Germans, thinking they were headed for Crich, would actually find themselves at Bullbridge.

Everyone was also issued a gas mask; even babies were given a pink one with rabbit ears. Mam came with us to the school to collect them, and we were each fitted with a contraption that had a rubber face piece, a hard cellophane window, and a snout-like protuberance at the front. The end of the snout contained a filter that would remove any poison gas we might draw in as we breathed. The masks had a strong smell of rubber, and I found mine claustrophobic. They were presented to us in little square boxes for which we bought a square case with straps so we could carry them over our shoulders; early in the war, policemen and air raid wardens often stopped us if we failed to carry our masks. Gradually, though, as the war ground on and the Germans didn't use poison gas (at least not on us), the cases more often than not held our lunch, and the mask was left on the hallstand at home. Mam also removed the lace curtains from the windowpanes.

And of course there were the sirens, 'Moaning Minnies' we called them, that could go off at any time of the day or night, their 'alert' sound undulating up and down like the cries of the tormented. I found this sound extremely frightening because I knew it meant enemy aircraft were close, and it would be well to take cover. Their departure was signalled by the sound of the 'all clear', a long, continuous wail. It was many years before a siren of any sort—police cars, ambulances, fire engines—failed to cause me a shiver of alarm.

For town dwellers, the sirens meant dressing hurriedly, grabbing a bag of provisions kept ready for the occasion, and sprinting to shelters that had been set up in the basements of large buildings, or under bridges, or, in London, the underground stations. In some cases, comparative safety lay at the end of the garden where prudent householders placed their Anderson shelters against such an emergency. These were supplied free to the poor and cost the more affluent seven pounds. They were named for their designer, Dr David Anderson, and consisted of a semi-circle of corrugated iron about eight feet long, rather like a Quonset hut, which the owner sank into the ground, leaving only the roof and the entrance door showing. To make it less conspicuous to the Luftwaffe, the householder piled soil on the roof, along with grass and other seeds. Inside there were built-in beds, along with a bucket to serve as a latrine. There was no source of light or heat so they were both dark and frigid, especially in winter. Flooding was also a big problem. Later, Herbert Morrison, then Minister of Home Security, introduced Morrison shelters for those without gardens. These had the advantage of being set up indoors under a table. They were table-shaped with wire at their sides, making them look like animal cages.

We country children were lucky in that we saw little of the dangerous side of war, and no one in our village built an air raid shelter. One farmer had his haystack set on fire by incendiary bombs dropped by a German pilot lightening his load as he fled back to Germany. One day, as I wheeled Gib towards the Tors in his pram, a Spitfire and a German bomber weaved together in the skies above us, and suddenly both baby and pram were silvered over with little strips of tinfoil that fell from the air. It was a complete mystery to all of us at the time, but we learned later that the Luftwaffe dropped the strips in an effort to make our Radar inoperable. This method of surveillance, now used at airports to monitor incoming planes, had just been invented. Later in the war, when I happened to be staying at my grandmother's in Matlock, a stray German bomber flew over the town peppering the area with machine gun bullets and dropping bombs on nearby Masson Hill. We all—Granny, Gladys, Jack, and me—hastened down to the cellar to take cover; I knew it was what London children had to do every night, and I felt very heroic. Bud came home from the pub shortly thereafter and wanted to know what we silly buggers thought we were doing down there. Sheepishly, we crept out of our hiding place and back up the stairs to the window, where we watched the rest of the Luftwaffe contingent limping home. We heard later that a lot of damage had been done when they bombed Derby station that night, and also Chatsworth House, home of the Duke and Duchess of Devonshire.

For children of the cities, it was a different story. London, Birmingham, Sheffield, Manchester, Coventry, Glasgow, and other large towns were savagely bombed, some of them night after night, and everyone had to get what sleep they could in shelters. On many nights we heard German bombers as they flew over on their way to Manchester or Birmingham. These aircraft had a different sound from our British planes; we all described it as a pig-like grunt. (The denigration of all things German had become a national pastime.) A friend told me warningly that, in order to find their way, the bombers were probably 'following the wires': the high-tension, electric wires that undulated above the field next to Ballantrae House and gave off tell-tale sparks in the damp air. 'Aren't you frightened?' she asked me. 'I should be!'

One day in 1940, outside my grammar school, a girl, her face a mask of despair, informed us that 'Frahnce has given in!' For some reason I remember that she used the long 'a'. I looked over towards Masson Hill and imagined barbed wire strung along its crest and all of us herded up there by Nazi storm troopers. I'm not sure what my rationale was for having the Germans put us on top of a hill, but that is the picture that came to my mind. Unfortunately, the song about our determination to 'hang out the washing on the Siegfried line' had been overturned, and the Maginot Line was where the laundry had ended up. The French had surrendered, and the British were in full retreat towards the French coast.

Britain was now alone, without much in the way of arms (the Home Guard, in its early days, drilled with broomsticks); we seemed essentially defenceless. This was when Churchill made one of his magnificent, heartening speeches: 'We shall fight on the seas and oceans…We shall fight on the landing grounds, we shall fight in the fields and in the streets, we shall fight in the hills. We shall never surrender'. On hearing this, Mam gave the wireless one of her sceptical looks. 'Oh, aye?' she said. Nevertheless, Churchill's words were spine-stiffening, even if there was little to back them up.

After the retreat of our army from Dunkirk in June of 1940, there was a lull. My parents thought it was the end: we were defeated, and the Germans would be on our doorstep at any moment. I hotly denied this: as the song told us, Britons never (never, never), shall be slaves. I believed it, but I was now twelve, old enough to know what dire straits we were in, and secretly, I was afraid. Nevertheless, I spent many hours constructing scenarios in which I bravely clobbered any Nazi foolish enough to try invading Fritchley.

In July 1940 came the beginning of the Battle of Britain, and we were heartened when our fighter pilots, Churchill's 'first of the few', won a series of dogfights against the Luftwaffe. These young fighter pilots became our heroes. They were mostly very young—some of them no more than eighteen or nineteen. One of them, Paddy Finucane, a young Irishman, became my particular hero, and on a Scottish holiday, I spent an hour carving his name and a shamrock on the bridge that spanned the local burn. Sometime later a newspaper headline read: 'Paddy's Bought It.' Finucane had been lost over Cap Finisterre off the Normandy coast. I sobbed for a week. 'For goodness' sake, Bren, you didn't even know the lad!' Mum protested. ('Bought it' was RAF slang for shot down; later their phrase was 'gone for a Burton'. A Burton was a brand of beer; it was as though the airman had strolled over to the pub for a drink and had failed to return.)

Meanwhile, in the Derwent Valley and throughout the country, many businesses had turned to making whatever was needed to wage war. Ironically, the war was to be the saving of the many local companies that had been struggling through the Depression years. Even before the end of the 1920s, local cotton manufacturers had begun to lose business as it slipped away to Lancashire with its handy seaports at Liverpool and Manchester. However, with the coming of war, the local cotton industry once more became busy making uniform materials in khaki, air force blue, and marine navy. The miners, too, whose job was to produce the coal needed in smelting and in the generation of electricity, were now ordered to work double shifts, as were the women called up to work in the bomb factories, including the one where Gladys eventually ended up near my grandmother's house in Matlock. The farmers, used to hard work, laboured even harder to produce the foods we had difficulty bringing in from the other side of world, and daylight savings time was doubled so that they were able to work in their fields until eleven at night.

The hydros had been failing as their number of clientele diminished; now they lost even more business because of the war and were forced to turn to other things. Rockside Hydro, for example, was taken over by the War Office and became a convalescent hospital for members of the armed services. Uncle George, who had been wounded in France, was at Rockside for a while. Smedley's Hydro became a venue for the intelligence services; the actor Dirk Bogard was one of the trainees there. The locals later called it 'the Kremlin'.

The Blitz on London began in earnest in September 1940 and continued for fifty-seven consecutive nights. All the big towns were now defended with Ack-Ack (anti-aircraft guns) and barrage balloons, which had no engines and were tethered with steel cables here and there throughout the towns in order to keep German bombers from coming in low to attack their targets more closely. Derby had its Ack-Ack and barrage balloons; Rolls Royce engines for RAF planes were made there.

Thousands of children, and other vulnerable citizens, had been evacuated to the countryside with the outbreak of war, but with the bombing even more people left the towns, including very young children, often without their mothers. It was later estimated that half of all British children, and a quarter of all citizens, moved out of the towns during the war. Whole schools were sometimes evacuated, along with their teachers. One such school shared space with Strutt's School pupils in Belper for the duration of the war.

The billeting of children was a haphazard affair depending on decisions made by the local authorities; moreover it was compulsory to accept a child if you had room for one. Some town officials had the children line up in the town square and families would come to take their pick, rather as if it were a slave market. In other areas, officials chose the family that was to be host to each child, sometimes placing little East Enders with middle-class families who had no idea how to cope with them—and vice versa. Auntie

Rose, my father's sister, who lived in Belper, was sent a little boy to look after. She had no children of her own, and when the child began peeing in her fireplace, she insisted he be sent elsewhere. Several refugee children came to Fritchley, where most of them fit in well with their host families.

Many of these youngsters had never been in the country-side before, had never seen a cow, or a sheep. A story that was passed round at the time concerned a small child from the slums of London who was evacuated to a local village. Having spotted a lark hovering above a field, he exclaimed: 'Look at 'im! 'E can't get up and 'e can't get down, and blimey 'e ain't 'alf 'ollerin'!' A Durward cousin, Uncle Eric's youngest daughter, was sent up to Derbyshire to live with her grandmother in Matlock when the Germans began bombing Plymouth. She didn't last long in the safety of the country town; she was lonely for her family, and 'I wants me dog!' was her plaintive cry. After a while, despite the bombing, she drifted back to her home, as did many children from other bombed cities.

Aunt Gladys had been 'courting' with Tom Moreton from about the time she came to live with us at Ambergate. Tom was one of three brothers who, with their father, ran a house-painting concern that was based in Cromford marketplace. Tom, a sturdily built man of middle height, had dark hair, blue eyes, and an imp-ish grin. He was always kind to us children, buying us the huge chocolate Easter eggs from Gladys's sweetshop before it closed down, and bringing us other little gifts from time to time. Mam disapproved of him: he owned a motorbike, and before the war he and Gladys would roar off in a cloud of exhaust, the brothers and their girls in pursuit, Mam tut-tutting in the background. I suppose Tom seemed a sort of Hell's Angel to her, although Hell's Angels hadn't yet come on the scene. Gladys took no notice of Mam's disapproval, and eventually she and Tom married.

After war was declared, Tom received his calling-up papers and enlisted in the army. At first, he was able to come on leave from time to time in his hairy khaki uniform, carrying the rifle that he would store, unloaded, under the bed he shared with Gladys. This didn't suit Mam, either. What if the kiddies got hold of it? What then? The kiddies were too much in awe of the sheer, sinister power of that weapon to ever think of touching it. (Eventually, Mam became very fond of Tom, but it took a while.) While her husband was overseas, although women with no dependents were being called up, Gladys had still not received her summons, which was fortunate since, in August of 1940, my brother Gilbert was born, and my mother needed her help more than ever.

CHAPTER 25

Grammar School

Ernest Bailey's Secondary School

IN JANUARY OF 1940, I entered Ernest Bailey's Secondary School, Matlock, or EBSM. (We were known locally as the Ernest Bailey's Sausage Makers.) The school was housed in what had once been one of the many hydros scattered about the town. The other pupils of the First Form had begun their school careers the previous September, but that was the month war was declared, and Dad and Mam were thinking of sending us to Canada for the duration. '*I'm* not running away!' said I. Gladys was to go with us, my mother told me—I'm not sure what Gladys's reaction was to this arrangement, although it was probably similar to mine. However, my parents decided against sending us into exile after seventy or more children drowned when the ship 'The City of

Benares' was torpedoed on its way to Canada. There was no more talk of evacuation after that terrible event.

I had taken the exam for Ernest Bailey's the summer before war broke out and, not surprisingly, considering my deficiencies in maths, had failed to pass. Only Joe Smith and a girl named Marion Outram passed that year from Fritchley and went on to Strutt's Grammar School. There was no coaching for the exam, so we were each on our own, although Joe had both his school-teacher mother and his Uncle Bill, who was also a teacher, to help. The only exam question I can remember answering had to do with a soldier standing on guard and at the same time eating a custard tart. An officer approached, and the soldier hid the tart inside his helmet. What, we were asked, would happen next?

What daft 'aporths they were, asking a question like that! 'It would drip all over his face, and he would be court martialled,' I replied. I probably gave a Mam-like sniff as I put down my pen.

Unfortunately this reply, and no doubt others equally naive, didn't get me into grammar school, which meant either that I would have to leave school at fourteen and start earning a living, 'twining it in' as the local phrase had it, or else Dad would have to pay the school fees. Fortunately, he was able to pay, and to my delight I was registered to go to Bailey's a few months after war was declared. A fellow pupil from Fritchley School, Elizabeth Lynam, had also been entered at Bailey's as a paying student. Her start had been delayed because of the war, but as soon as Mam and Dad decided that I should begin school in January, Elizabeth's parents took the plunge and decided to send Elizabeth too, so that 'Lib' Lynam and I continued to be schoolmates. Clad, at last, in a gymslip and blouse, long lisle stockings held up with suspenders attached to my liberty bodice, and a brimmed velour hat with the Bailey's badge at the front, I met Elizabeth at the top of Fritchley Lane each morning to walk the mile and a half to the Crich market place, where at eight o'clock we boarded the blue Midland General bus to Matlock.

At school we had several very good teachers. There was the French Master, a slight, handsome man with a small moustache. All of us girls were in love with him, although he shortly had to leave for the air force. Afterwards, how we giggled and squirmed when he visited wearing his blue uniform with the RAF wings on his chest. A very Francophile mistress, Miss Cressley, came out of retirement to teach French in his place. She was in love with Paris, and if we were lucky, she would talk about that city for the entire fifty-minute period. Miss Eastwood taught us English Literature and was also Head Mistress. We studied *Macbeth* with her, poetry from *The Golden Treasury*—Keats, Shelley, Wordsworth—the Brontë novels, and Siegfried Sassoon's *Memoirs of a Foxhunting Man*, among many other works. The rumour at the school was that Miss Eastbourne had been engaged to Rupert Brooke (the poet who died during the Great War), and this explained her maiden state. Since then, however, I have met two other women who told me that their English teachers had been engaged to Rupert Brooke, so it was obviously a widespread, and false, rumour developed by romantic little girls. Unfortunately, the Art Mistress, Miss Bailey (no relation to Ernest), although she was a good artist herself, was afraid of her pupils, and we did pretty much what we wanted in her classes. The History Mistress was a good influence—I had a schoolgirl crush on her, probably because she had a steel-trap mind and a great sense of humour. She was a rather ugly woman. Pretty and red-haired, the Domestic Science Mistress was friendly to and popular with the other girls, but to me, she was cool and sometimes downright hostile. This puzzled me until I happened to mention her name at home. 'Oh, her!' said Mam, which is when the story came to light that she was the woman who had been Dad's girlfriend until Mam 'ran her off' at a dance at a nearby village.

After a while, this Domestic Science Mistress left to go into one of the women's services, and another woman took her place, who I think, in retrospect, was sadistic or mentally disturbed. On the rare occasions when we had enough sugar and margarine from home to make a cake, she would force us to beat these together by hand, which in that ice-cold school kitchen could take the better part of an hour. The previous teacher had allowed us to warm our ingredients near the stove. This substitute teacher also insisted that we pronounce the word roughage (as in fibre) as 'roo-haage' and became almost apoplectic when some brave soul pointed out that this was incorrect.

The school was equipped with two laboratories, science being taught by Mr Ridge (physics) and Mr Dredge (chemistry and botany). Mr Ridge was a tall, dry, precise man who, after he had mistakenly mixed two chemicals together that had caused a piece of lab equipment to collapse, explained to us that it had not *ex*ploded, but had *im*ploded. He was very insistent on this point. In Mr Dredge's lab, we played about with iron filings, which seems to have been *de rigueur* for the times, and were also allowed to fool with mercury, pushing about poisonous little balls of it on our desks. Today this would be looked upon with horror. I'm sorry to say that I learned almost nothing of science from Mr Ridge, except that it is possible to implode something, and the information that the atom is indivisible. In the latter case, unfortunately for all of us, a few years later, circumstances proved him to be wrong.

The Gym Mistress, Miss Creamer, was like an overgrown schoolgirl herself, a tall, bony woman. At school she wore an extremely short gymslip, long black stockings, and black bloomers, in one elasticized leg of which she kept her handkerchief. It was quite usual to see her pause in the middle of the playground, haul her hanky out of her bloomers, give a hearty blow, and then stuff it back again. We had a good gym at the school, and I soon learned to leap over the box and the horse, to hang upside-down on the parallel bars, and generally fling myself about. My arms were weak, however, and I never managed to haul myself to the top of the ropes.

Miss Creamer also taught us country and ballroom dancing in the gym, the taller girls taking the man's part. I was one of the tall ones and in later years always tried to take charge when ballroom dancing; most of my partners didn't like their roles to be usurped, and this led to some tussles on the dance floor. We had parties at the end of term, especially before Christmas, but no boys were present, and we danced with one another. Sometime later, when Jo Crisp and I went to dances at the drill hall in Matlock, it was quite usual to see women dancing together if no man had asked them. Women never asked men to dance in those days, except during what was called a 'ladies' excuse me', which was the only time women were allowed to cut in.

I was quite good at games, and although I was not a very fast runner, I found myself playing centre half with the school's hockey team and centre forward in our games of basketball. The school had no playing fields of its own, and we often borrowed the town of Matlock's football field. When this was not available, we took the train to Cromford to play on the meadows, close to Richard Arkwright's mansion alongside the River Derwent.

Because of the war, we had no master or mistress to teach us music. Instead the geography mistress took over the music class, during which she beat out the rhythm of a tune, and we were expected to guess what it was. It made for a long, boring lesson and imparted very little about music.

At Bailey's, boys and girls were segregated throughout the school and had no classes together at all. The only time we got together with the boys was when travelling to and from Matlock. Roughly a dozen children joined the bus at Holloway, Common End, and Lea Bridge, among them Jo Crisp, who became a lifelong friend. There was the usual banter back and forth, including grousing about 'Kong' (Mr Orme, the Headmaster, was nicknamed King Kong), and the usual taunts about who 'goes with' whom. For a time, there was speculation that Brenda Wallis was going with a youth named Tom Millar who joined the bus at Common End with his sister. This probably started after Tom told me one morning on the bus that I 'looked like a film star.' (Another youth suggested he meant Minnie Mouse.) There was much catcalling back and forth across the street about this as we walked from the bus to school, but that's as far as it went. Girls and boys of our class and age, eleven to seventeen, seldom dated. It was different for those whose schooling ended at fourteen. These children entered the working world early and were often courting by the time they were fifteen and married before they were twenty.

In the way children today have television, we had the wireless. We often compared notes about our favourite programs on the morning bus. 'Did you hear ITMA last night?' was the query most weeks. ITMA, an acronym for *It's That Man Again*, starred comedian Tommy Handley and involved a great many characters: Funf, for instance, who was supposed to be an announcer on German radio, delivered terrible threats to the British and ended darkly with 'Funf has spoken' in a thick, supposedly German, accent. He was portrayed as inept and was repeatedly hit by bombs. 'Vot voss dot?' he would gasp. 'Dot voss a bombff?' There was also a char, that is, a cleaning woman, named Mrs Mopp who would enter the studio at inappropriate times to ask Handley, 'Can I do you now, sir?' The farewell 'TTFN,' a phrase taken over by Tigger in the Disney version of 'Winnie the Pooh', was another ITMA acronym meaning 'ta ta for now'. We children loved Tommy Handley, as did many adults, probably because he kept us laughing when there was very little to laugh about. When he died, just after the war, he was given a funeral procession, his cortege driven slowly through the streets of London with thousands lining the route. I'm happy to say that there was no avalanche of flowers and teddy bears left at the gates of the BBC.

There were other BBC shows, such as 'Monday Night at Eight' and 'Much Binding in the Marsh', which starred Arthur Askey and Richard Murdoch, who, fifty years on, appeared in the '90s TV show, 'Rumpole of the Bailey'. All these shows we avidly discussed on the morning bus.

Also talked about (and imitated) was an Englishman who had defected to the Nazis and was working for the German prop-aganda machine. He had an extremely upper-class accent, hence his nickname, 'Lord Haw Haw.' 'Gahmany calling; Gahmany calling,' he would announce, his voice breaking into the BBC programming; he would go on to tell us how badly we were los-ing and encourage us to surrender. We found him hilarious and looked upon him with scorn.

On the bus, if adults were standing, we children were expected to give them our seats. If we didn't, and someone complained to Kong, we'd be harangued about it for fifteen minutes after morn-ing prayers. Usually, the boys stood and we girls doubled up, one girl sitting on another's knee. If we didn't, a prefect, who had some power over children in the lower forms, would order us out of our seats. We didn't mind doing this for older people but resented having to stand for the mill girls who were not a deal older than we were. It didn't occur to us that we were privileged in that we could continue our schooling and weren't obliged to labour at the mill the minute we turned fourteen.

When we disembarked at Matlock near the train station on what is now the beginning of the ring road round the town, we re-segregated ourselves so that when we got to Lime Tree Walk which runs from Bank Road up to the school, the boys walked on the right-hand pavement and we girls on the left. We wouldn't see each other again, except from a distance, until we threw ourselves onto the home-going bus at four-fifteen.

If I closed my eyes, fudged it a little, and pretended it was an all-girls school, Bailey's was just like the St Ethelred's of the school stories. We wore uniforms, winter and summer. In winter, it was a navy blue gymslip and white blouse, a navy blazer, and a beret or brimmed hat, both of which bore the school's insignia. I was rather disappointed in the Bailey's gymslip, having hoped for one with two box pleats fore and aft, similar to the one that Margaret wore at Strutt's. Instead, we had to wear a white blouse and a tie with our A-line, sleeveless tunic in navy blue rayon, along with long black lisle stockings. It was only slightly like the uniform sported by the girls of St Ethelred's. In summer I wore a cotton dress in blue and white, accompanied by white socks and sandals. Mum made the dress from the only material available in wartime: a vivid blue cotton with a pattern of white parallelograms. Pete jeered that they made me look like a packet of soap flakes. Winter and summer our overcoat was a gabardine Mac. The gymslips and dresses had to last for two or three years and eventually became both tight and short.

Like St Ethelred's, the school was divided into houses, in our case Celts, Romans, Mercians, and Danes, in keeping with the various groups from the continent that, over the centuries, had invaded the British Isles and settled in the area. I had hoped to join the Celts since my name was Wallis (not quite the same as the Scottish Wallace, perhaps, but close) and was indignant when, because the Danes were short of members, I was allocated to the Dane House and had to wear an embroidered Viking ship on my blazer instead of a thistle. A song, written by one of the masters, went:

Celts, Romans, Mercians, Danes are we,
Who, though our childhood days are spent in learning's way,
Stride forth in manly [!] rivalry.
And as we march, our banner shall proclaim
The faith, the loyalty that knows no shame.

Another ditty always sung at the end of term, and to which we included a note of gloom when we sang lines three and four, went:

Lord dismiss us with thy blessing,
All who here shall meet no more.
Those returning,
Those returning,
Make more faithful than before.

Unlike in schools today, we Ernest Bailey's Sausage Makers were never taught 'the facts of life', and it was left to ITMA to remind us of this omission when Tommy Handley's show produced yet another acronym: DYMETYA? It meant 'Did Your Mother Ever Tell You Anything?' On the bus, we girls confessed that the answer in most families was 'no', and although there were obscure hints from girls with more sophisticated parents, we on the bus never discussed sex. To my mother's obvious relief, I had assured her, when she had tentatively brought up the subject, that I knew everything there was to know about 'babies and that stuff'. A school friend had told me that babies make their way into the womb if 'you kiss a boy when it's your time of the month'. She had also informed me with equal authority that 'babies come out through your belly button'. Margaret had proven to be a little less ignorant than either I or the girl on the subject, telling me that she had come across her parents in bed—'me Dad on top of me Mam'—which meant, she said, that she was going to have a sister or brother. Why else would her parents allow themselves to get into such an undignified position?

We from the small surrounding villages who came to school in the big town of Matlock were further enlightened by a more sophisticated girl whose mother was French. This explained, we told each other, her superior knowledge in matters concerning reproduction. The girl lived in Matlock, but one day she cornered us on our way to catch our bus in order to show us an extremely salacious poem. Shamefaced, we read this offering, giggling and nudging one another the while. After we had all taken a turn to read the poem, one of my bus-mates told the depraved Frenchy 'You're dirty!', after which we ran off to catch our bus. It was a subdued journey home.

Then there was. Margaret had never mentioned it to me, and one day, after Mum asked me if she or the girls at school had 'said anything' about it, and I admitted they hadn't, she took me up to her bedroom. 'Bren, you must tell me if you bleed', she began. I, having no clue what she was talking about, looked at her blankly; however she finally got through to me that before too long (I was twelve) I might find blood in my knickers. When I did, she would have rags for me to pin to an elastic belt with two large safety pins front and back. (Hence our phrase 'she's got her rags on' when a girl was bad-tempered.) This may seem a primitive arrangement, but tampons came in only after the war, and the rather bulky sanitary napkins were used only by the more worldly wise—which Mum was not. I began to buy these for myself after I received my first paycheck, although only if there was a female behind the counter at Boots', and then only if she was at least forty years old. At the end of my interview with Mum, I was convinced that this bleeding business would happen only once and that would be that. How mistaken I was; no wonder we referred to our monthly menses as 'the curse'.

Having all this new knowledge of the human anatomy told, or rather hinted, to us, was a sign that we were becoming what people nowadays refer to as teenagers. In the forties we were very different from today's youngsters. To begin with, we were not called teenagers, since the term had not yet been coined, but were referred to as either girls, or boys, until we reached our twenty-first birthday when, miraculously, the boys became men, and the girls remained…girls. My grandmother often introduced me to strangers as 'Cis's girl'. During these early adolescent years, some girls developed what we called 'crushes' on another girl, usually a best friend, and it was acceptable for such couples to walk along the street holding hands. I believe now, that with the exception of girls who were genuinely Lesbian, these crushes were our way of hiding from the boys, who, although the same age as we were, seemed to be gangly little pests in short pants who, when they were not harassing us in some way, did little but fight and squabble among themselves. It was only later that some of us began to have boyfriends, even though the boys were still gangly and now had spots. We also differed from today's youngsters in that we girls used very little make-up and were not allowed to spend inordinate amounts of money on dress. We had become used to 'making do' during the war, which was only just over, and for a while still had to contend with a points system for clothes. Nor did we cling together fearfully when we thought of our more senior years when we would reach twenty-one and life would be over; most of us happily anticipated our adulthood.

About this time, my mother, who had had to grow up quickly as the eldest daughter of a working-class family, became worried that my more middle-class milieu was holding me back. One summer holiday she decided it was time I stopped looking like a little girl with my bobbed hair and arranged for me to have my first 'perm'. In working-class families at that time, girls of fifteen were not considered too young to be courting, and since I had no boyfriend, Mum, fearing that I must be backward in this regard, thought that a more sophisticated hairstyle might do the trick. The hairdresser ran her business at a house in Ambergate, and when the day came, I took a bus down to the valley from Fritchley Lane. The woman had her 'salon' in her front room, and to me it looked like a small torture chamber. After she had washed my hair, my beautician sat me down in a chair and began to douse my locks in a foul-smelling liquid before winding each one onto a fearsome-looking curler. As she finished each curl, she plugged the curler into a machine: a round disc fastened to the ceiling from which the curlers dangled. Afterwards she switched the contraption on and left me to cook amongst an intensifying chemical smell in order, she said, to get on with her 'Hoovering'.

The whole process took the better part of two hours, as I remember it, and the thought crossed my mind that I could end up bald. However, sounds of vacuuming finally died away, and the hairdresser came back to unhook me, comb out my curls, and leave me to admire myself in the mirror. I thought I looked a bobby dazzler. When I got home, however, Dad was livid with both my mother and me, and Miss Eastwood, the Head Mistress at Bailey's, gave me a look of absolute disgust when I appeared at school with my brand new 'hair do'. I was not in the least abashed; I thought it was lovely. Nowadays, if a granddaughter permed her hair at fifteen, I'd be appalled. Come to think of it, that's not strictly true; I'd just be glad she hadn't dyed it green or shaved it off altogether.

By this time, 'Mam' had metamorphosed into 'Mum'. This was because at Bailey's I had noticed that calling my mother Mam had begun to sound lower-class, whereas Mum, or better yet Mummy, was classier. I didn't dare call her Mummy to her face; she would have laughed and rolled her eyes. As she would have done if I had started to say 'excuse me' whenever I sneezed, although I had learned that this was the *politesse* expected by the families of the more upper-class girls. The class system was obviously getting to me.

CHAPTER 26

The War Continues

Uncle Gib, Home Guard; cousin Bert Dewar, King's Own Scottish Borderers

EARLY IN THE WAR, several of my Durward uncles were called up. The first, Uncle Eric, who lived in Plymouth, was in the army overseas at some point. Uncle Reg, already a member of the Royal Army Medical Corps (the RAMC), was sent to France in the early years of the war and took part in the retreat at Dunkirk, carrying wounded men from the beach to the fleet of small boats that had braved the Channel to take them home. Because of his work on the beaches, Uncle Reg suffered from a weak heart for the rest of his life. Uncle George, also in the army, was wounded at Caen during the 1940 retreat. Uncle Bud, the farmer, was in a reserved occupation. However, Jack, who was seventeen in 1941 and working at Burgon's food shop in Crown Square, was now close to the age when he would inevitably receive his calling-up papers. Poor Grandmother was distraught. Most of her boys were abroad somewhere, and she was terrified that they would come for Jack, 'me lad' as she called him. "E's too young!' she kept saying, but 'they' were now beginning to call up boys as young as seventeen and a half. To me, twelve years old and eager to 'get into the war' as I put it (what fools young mortals be), was envious of Jack's superior age. Today I think that recruiting seventeen-year-olds is as criminal as giving a gun to a child in napkins.

Eventually Jack received his call-up papers. He joined the RAF ground staff and looked so handsome in his blue uniform that I was beside myself with envy. Later, he was sent overseas to Malta, Cyprus, and then to Italy.

Of family members who served overseas, only Bert Dewar, Dad's Scottish cousin, failed to return. He was killed shortly after D-Day in 1944 and was buried in Normandy. During the war we also lost Dad's brother, Arnold, from natural causes, and in Scotland Granny's sister, Aunt Rose. These were my first losses of family through death, and for a long time, I was inconsolable. By now, women were being called up, but Gladys continued to be exempt, possibly because she was a soldier's wife and was also helping Mum, who had given birth to brother Gib. However, at some point later in the war, the sisters quarrelled. I never knew what it was about, but Gladys's name was not to be mentioned in the house; 'You'll have to pull your weight, young lady', Mum told me. It is true that I'd had an easy ride on the domestic front with Gladys a part of the immediate family, and on Sunday mornings I now found myself hanging out the new baby's nappies on the line, or peeling the spuds for dinner, instead of walking with Dad over Windy Gap and down to Whatstandwell to visit my grandparents.

Happily, I didn't lose sight of Gladys, who had become a good friend. She and I were only ten years apart in age, rather less than the age gap between Gladys and my mother. On school days in Matlock, I was in the habit of walking up to my grand-mother's for a dinner of a baked potato and occasionally a slice of Spam; Gladys, who was living at home again, was often there too. As soon as she stopped working for my mother, she had been recruited to work in an old wool factory near Grandmother's house that had been taken over by the government and was now producing bombs. At first, she appeared remote, even a little tough, with her overall, her cigarette, and her hair done up in the regulation turban, but after an initial awkwardness, we were as friendly as ever. Meanwhile, Mam was interviewing other young women, looking for Gladys's replacement. She never found one, possibly because she was offering a salary only about half of what they could earn at Smedley's, the dye works, or in the armament factories. Moreover, women were now being taken a little more seriously and, because so many men were away in the forces, entrusted with 'men's jobs', which meant they were beginning to feel empowered at last. Poor Mum began to realize how well off she had been with Gladys to help.

The war dragged on. There were high and low spots, although we were never quite so sunk in gloom as the winter after Dunkirk, when between 1940 and '41, a great deal of shipping was lost to German U-boats in the Atlantic and the winter was dark, snowy, foggy, and unusually cold for Britain. We were still alone against the Nazis, until December 1941 when the Japanese attacked Pearl Harbor, and America was dragged into the war over protests from many German-Americans and members of the Isolationist movement. 'About time!' was then my reaction; now I've changed that to 'Thank goodness!' I doubt we'd have made it without the Yanks.

In the summer of 1941, Germany invaded the USSR and thereby, like Napoleon, made a fatal mistake. At first Hitler was successful; Leningrad (St Petersburg) and Moscow were besieged and reduced to rubble; nevertheless the Russian people defended themselves with enormous bravery. This was when they became known as 'our gallant Russian allies', although only a year before they had been Hitler's friends and therefore fiends incarnate. In December, the Russians mounted a counter-attack, and as the winter set in, the Germans began their inevitable retreat; the tide of war had turned. During this time, the Russians and their admirers called for Britain to open a 'second front', that is, to attack the Germans via France and the Low Countries, presumably to take pressure off the Russian army so they could drive the

Nazis even further west. Churchill was too canny to order such an invasion until he saw how far the Russians advanced before the German army stopped them; friend or foe, he didn't want to see Russians on our doorstep just across the channel. We would deal with the Nazis in France, but later.

Instead, in 1942 the Allies landed in North Africa, where Hitler was by now firmly ensconced. Gladys's Tom was there, as we discovered when we found a photo of him in a magazine, helping to remove ammunition from the back of a truck 'somewhere overseas'. Troops abroad were forbidden to tell their relatives where they were, and censorship was fierce; censors opened every letter from abroad, and most soldiers were careful not to put themselves in danger. We at home were also admonished to keep troop movements quiet. Every railway station and train had its picture of Hitler with his hand to his ear above the words 'You Never Know Who May Be Listening!' Another showed a sinking merchant ship along with the words 'Careless talk costs lives'. After many reverses—we almost lost North Africa—thousands of Italians and Germans surrendered, and Rommel's Afrika Korps was finally defeated. At the same time, German forces continued to retreat westward from Russia, the U-boat war was won in the Atlantic, and a little later the Allies landed in Italy. (Cousin Bert Dewar was there with the King's Own Scottish Borderers.) The Italians shortly surrendered, but the Germans continued to fight all the way from the toe to the top of Italy's boot.

Surprisingly, we had a couple of holidays away from home during the war. Most seaside holidays were not possible because much of the British coastline was bristling with gun emplacements and was off-limits to civilians, but one year Dad, Pete, and I travelled up to Scotland by train, followed a week later by Mum, who had left Beryl and Gib at home with Gladys. (This was before the sisters quarrelled.) I felt guilty about this wartime expedition but nevertheless happy to be north of the border once again. At Newton Stewart station, Peter and I waited two hours for our mother's train to come in, only to find that it had been shunted into a siding to allow the troop trains to pass that were headed for ships waiting in the harbour at Stranraer. I spent the time feeling guilty because I was able to take a holiday while those on the troop train were off to face death.

We took our bikes with us to Scotland that year and found the countryside, as in Derbyshire, clotted with troop-filled lorries on the roads and soldiers milling about at every station, their boots thudding against the wooden platforms, their guns and packs weighing them down. 'Bloody civilians!' I heard one murmur to his pal. On another occasion, I went north with Aunt Flo and her new husband, Ted, this time riding in the guard's van since there was no other room for us on the train. The carriages were blacked out, but since the locomotives ran on coal and produced copious sparks that could be seen for miles, we were lucky the Luftwaffe didn't spot us.

Throughout my childhood, Scotland to me was heaven. Before petrol rationing, we often drove up there, and the first thing I did on arrival at Uncle Gib and Auntie Rose's Polbae cottage was take myself off to the woods and the little bridge over the brown waters of the burn. There, I would run along the path beside the stream to my favourite trees and embrace them as if they were loved relatives. To me it was as though the trees hugged me back. Later, I pulled on my rubber boots and walked the moor, glorying in the sweep of it, the little lochs, the Galloway hills rising on the horizon, the thrilling scent of heather and bog myrtle. As we left to drive home to Derbyshire, I would invariably be weeping in the back seat of the car; 'Is she blubbing yet?' Dad would ask as we began the drive home. I felt I had every reason to blub; we were going back to dull old Derbyshire, where there were too many people and the hills were not nearly so grand. It makes me laugh to think of my dramatic young self; now that I am far away from it Derbyshire has become my Mecca, although I have given up hugging trees.

Towards the end of my years at Bailey's, Pete joined me there and walked with me to Crich market place every morning to catch our bus. Lib Lynam had left the school when she finished Form Four, much to the Head's disgust; she had taken the place of a child who might have continued on, he told her parents, even as far as college. Beryl, when she was of grammar-school age, found a place at the Convent School in Belper; Gib, in his turn, went to Alfreton Grammar—by then, all children continued schooling until they were at least sixteen. But for me, the end of school was in sight, and soon it would be time to start twining it in.

Meanwhile, thousands of American troops were entering the British Isles, plus thousands more from the colonies, as well as Free French, Poles, and other free Europeans who were being mustered and trained for the coming invasion of France. As the number of foreign troops in the country continued to increase, we began to joke that the British Isles would be lucky if they didn't sink.

On June 6, 1944, when we were in the midst of an English lesson with Miss Eastwood, the Headmaster came striding into the classroom, his face mottled with excitement, his black gown billowing about him like wings. 'Our troops have invaded France!' he announced, and *Macbeth* was pushed aside for the rest of the hour. None of us was surprised by the news: rumours of a huge build-up of troops along the south coast had been spreading for months, and many nights it had been impossible to sleep as thousands of RAF and American bombers thundered overhead on their way to pound France and Germany. Afraid but hopeful, we looked at each other: was this the beginning of the end?

Shortly after the invasion of France, we children of the Fifth Form were faced with 'school cert', the final exam that would give us our leaving certificate and perhaps determine whether we went on to the sixth form and subsequently university. I studied hard and passed in every subject, even maths, and felt myself ready for the big world; my parents never contemplated the possibility that I might go on to University. Very few children at the school did so, although the boys were much more likely to continue their studies than were the girls. The thinking at home was now that I had been 'educated', it was time for me to decide what I was going to do to fill in the time before I married. Any extra money should go towards the boys' education; Gib was still at Fritchley School, Pete at Bailey's, and my mother, along with most parents of their kind, thought education more important for their sons because 'they'll have families to support'. I have no idea what my father's views were, but I assume he agreed because he didn't intervene as he had when he had decided I should attend Grammar School. No one, in either family, had ever attended a university. Both my parents hoped the boys would get some sort of office job, but any idea of further education for me never entered their minds. This thinking about gender roles was pretty universal of our class at the time. I secretly rebelled against it but felt compelled to accept the theory; now I realize that I ought to have screamed bloody murder as a modern teen would have done and insisted on more schooling, especially after it became clear that neither Pete nor Gib would be going on to college.

So, what was I going to do? Jobs had become available at Matlock library, which the Council had opened in a house at the bottom of Steep Turnpike. But this was shortly before D-Day, when I was still convinced I could wait until I was seventeen and then volunteer for the Women's Auxiliary Air Force. In the WAAF the women acted as office workers, drivers, and mechanics; only a few of them flew—usually taking planes from one airfield to another within Britain. Piloting a plane over Germany had been part of the daydream that now began to fade as reality took over. (It's amusing to remember how afraid I was of flying when I first took to the air in 1960.) In any case, with victory a possibility, it was likely the war would be won before I was sent my calling-up papers, and I decided that if there was no war to fight, why bother? The Headmaster was angry because I hadn't applied for the library job, telling me I would have been taken on immediately as a library junior, a sort of apprentice—a position that had now gone to another girl. However, the County Library in Derby was also advertising for juniors to join their staff, and one day Dad drove me down to Library Headquarters in St Mary's Gate near Derby Cathedral, for an interview. I was successful and the next week began work in their cataloguing department.

I liked the work and the people; it was the surroundings I objected to. I was a country girl and unused to towns—Matlock was the largest town I had ever been in for any length of time— and I felt hemmed in by the traffic and the smoke-blackened buildings. The library was housed in a ramshackle, Dickensian old building with odd nooks and crannies that today I would probably love for its history. It held, in addition to a lending library, all the backroom facilities of library work for the county: cataloguing, classification, the ordering of books, and their delivery to schools and branch libraries throughout the Derbyshire. It was my job to learn all these tasks. At the same time, I took night classes at Derby Tech that would lead to professional qualifications. My desk had a view down St Mary's Gate to the Cathedral; nevertheless, I felt cabined, cribbed, confined. Work was infinitely more constricting than school had ever been, and my days were long. On winter mornings, before the sun was above the horizon, I walked down the Bottom Hag to Ambergate station, a distance of about a mile and a half, to catch the 8.10 to Derby. I left the train at Nottingham Road and walked another mile or so to the Headquarters building. In the evening I caught the 5.30 train and reversed the process. Walking up the Bottom Hag in the dark of winter took roughly three-quarters of an hour, and I was seldom home before 6.30. For this I was paid ten shillings a week with two weeks' holiday a year. Despite its interest, working life came to me as a shock.

CHAPTER 27

The War Is Over!

Winston Churchill

ON THE MORNING OF 8 May 1945, as I walked down the lane on the way to catch my train to Derby, Mr Rollinson, leaning over his garden gate, stopped me. 'It's over, Brenda', he informed me solemnly. 'Everybody's got a holiday.' I thanked him, turned, and walked back home. For me, the end of five years of war was as prosaic as that.

In London and other big cities, there were wild celebrations with people dancing in the streets and kissing total strangers. In the East End, the Cockneys came out to do a knees-up, and people crowding the area outside Buckingham Palace were rewarded when 'Winnie' appeared on the balcony with the King, Queen, and the two princesses, Elizabeth in her ATS uniform, to wave to the crowds.

We heard about all this on the wireless. In Fritchley, there was a bonfire that evening, but I didn't go to it; I felt strangely numb, as though I had been living in the midst of noise, excitement, and fear, and suddenly it was all gone, as though a gong had been struck repeatedly for the last five years and now was stilled, its reverberations dying away, becoming ever more faint.

Victory over the Japanese—VJ Day— came on 15 August 1945, after America dropped atomic bombs on Hiroshima and Nagasaki. Many of us, not knowing what had been unleashed, were glad. We knew that thousands, perhaps even millions of our men, would have been killed had we invaded Japan, but now it was over, and soon our troops would come home. Only a few realized what a fiendish weapon we had unleashed upon the world. Hatred of all things German and Japanese ran deep, and many of us felt that the dropping of the atomic bombs on Japan, and the carpet-bombing of German towns, were no more than they deserved after the inhuman things they had done. It took me some years to dig myself out of that belief and admit that, although the Germans and Japanese had been unbelievably vicious, we, too, had often been driven to being less than civilized.

Immediately after the war, Churchill called a general election, and many of us were shocked and distressed when Clement Atlee's socialists defeated the Tory government. Churchill had been our hero, but the armed forces and members of the working class had decided they had had enough of 'nob' rule, or government by the upper classes, and felt that, with Clement Atlee, Nye Bevan, and Ernest Bevin in charge, the common man should have his turn. The new government was to enjoy only one term in office after they were blamed for the inevitable austerity that came after the war, when Britain suffered a time of gloom perhaps even worse than during the most disastrous years of the conflict. Then, patriotic feeling had been widespread, and we had all cheerfully 'done our bit': had dug for victory, sacrificed our saucepans and the railings round our front yards, and saved our empty tin cans to help make bombs and planes. We had managed with less food, fewer or no holidays, and no new clothes; we had fought and died, civilians as well as the fighting forces, and through it all had kept a 'stiff upper lip'. Now the war was over, and expectations were high, but millions on the continent were still suffering far worse than we, and it was to be at least four more years before we began to emerge from the effects of war.

What seemed the unkindest cut of all was when, instead of a sudden rush of supplies into the food shops, our rations were cut, and we had even less to eat than during the war. In September 1947 even potatoes and bread became rationed, as they had not been in wartime. Ships that had entered our ports carrying food among the guns and tanks were now diverted to the Continent in an attempt to feed the starving Europeans. Thirty to forty million people between Moscow and the west coast of France had been displaced from their homes and were wandering about in search of lost relatives, or food, or somewhere to call their own. These were people whose homes had been destroyed by bombing or shelling, or the passing by of armies. Some people, bewildered, emaciated, and hungry, had been suddenly released from prisoner of war or concentration camps, or had fled their own lands before the advancing Russian army. Germany had been reduced to rubble by Allied bombing, and starving people were eating dandelions, the bark of trees, and even oak leaves. Thousands of children were living on just a few hundred calories a day; all this while they and their families wandered constantly, looking for a place to settle. It was reported that one little displaced girl spent the first six years of her life on the road. But that little girl was one of the lucky ones; it was estimated that thirteen million children had been killed during the war.

Eventually, various countries built camps for these displaced people, or DPs, as they came to be called. There was one such camp outside Newton-Stewart in Scotland, a cluster of long, wooden, barrack-like huts plus a mess hall; some of the DPs must have felt they were back in prison camp. Eventually, some of the displaced people went home, but many found jobs in the surrounding countryside, on farms or as factory workers; some married local girls (or boys) and settled down. Britain's population was beginning to diversify, as it had not done for hundreds of years.

As time went on and our food continued to be rationed, many felt that the government was deliberately withholding food, and there was much talk of 'socialist austerity'. Meat was still scarce, and people were reduced to eating unusual foods such as whale steaks and snoek, a fish from the waters near South Africa. This, too, was blamed on the socialist government. One Minister in particular, Sir Stafford Cripps, was instrumental in introducing many of the necessary austerities of the time. The fact that he was inordinately thin and always had a severe expression didn't help, nor did the rumour of Churchill's deliberate slip of the tongue: 'Sir Stifford Crapps'. Five years after they took office, the socialist government was voted out, and Churchill was back in power.

I continued my work at the library, taking correspondence courses augmented by night classes at Derby Tech in cataloguing, classification, and the history of English literature. The latter I loved; the other two were not arduous, and I took and passed various exams. My work at the County Library Headquarters was interesting, and I made several friends among the employees, most of whom were young and had been recruited, as I had, from local grammar schools. One girl, Betty Thrupp—inevitably called Thruppence—was a particular friend. Some Saturday mornings, at the end of our five-and-a-half-day week, I rode my bike to the station, put it in the guard's van, and took the train to Derby as usual. After work, Thruppence and I would ride out of Derby and head for one of the youth hostels in the Peak District, where we had reserved beds. Sometimes we were joined by a group of young folk from Uttoxeter whom we had met on an earlier expedition. The hostels were sparse, providing a bed, a mattress, and a blanket; we took our own cotton sleeping bags. There was always a communal kitchen, where we prepared our suppers of beans on toast and our breakfasts of bacon and fried tomatoes. The bedrooms were icy, the beds lumpy, but we loved it nonetheless. One weekend—thrilling for me with my love of Scotland—Thruppence and I spent the night in Bonnie Prince Charlie's room at Hartington Hall, where the Prince was reputed to have slept during his invasion of England in 1745. He got no further south than Derby.

I was beginning to feel at home in Derby when, in 1946, I was asked to swap jobs with a girl named Angela Saddington, also from Fritchley, who had been working at Belper Library and now 'needed headquarters experience'. I was indignant. What, transferred into a backwater such as Belper, a sophisticated townie like me? Willy-nilly, I transferred, and began to enjoy myself once I had become reconciled. Like Matlock, Belper had been blessed with a philanthropic doctor who had willed his house on Bridge Street to be used as a library. The building was large, with a spacious, book-lined room downstairs, a reference/music room, and a corner that acted as the children's section. Upstairs could be found the staff room, more bookshelves, and areas where routine paperwork was done. Surrounding the building was a garden with its own gardener, Mr Nightingale, who from time to time presented us with bouquets of lilac in spring and boxes of vegetables in summer. The gardener (we never knew if he belonged to Florence Nightingale's family), was a curious old man who worked part-time for Allen's, a firm of undertakers. He came to work now and then wearing his black tailcoat and trousers, a tall top hat, and a lugubrious expression. He was going, he would tell us solemnly, to a 'fyoondrell'. He was also noted for his odd placement of aitches, and often spoke of 'Mr Hosborne's 'ydrangeas'. Mr Osborne was County Librarian and had persuaded Mr Nightingale to grow flowers as well as vegetables in the library garden. Our boss was very fond, the gardener told us, of 'hartichokes'.

The library's janitor was a young man just home from the army who clattered about the library in his old army boots. He was a cheerful soul who, having seen the first spring flowers, told us that the 'Crocus delecti' were in bloom. I don't think he was joking, and he did read a lot of mystery novels.

The staff at Belper consisted of a librarian, another junior, and two slightly older girls. There was also a children's librarian, Betty Tomlinson. Betty was older than us juniors and had been a WREN during the war working with radar. She and I became good friends. I was in charge of the desk and soon got to know all the local worthies, and those who were not so worthy. A great many of the women I thought of as old ladies—they were considerably younger than I am now—would come to the library every week, asking in their strong Derbyshire accents for 'luv boooks'. I would save their Ethel M Dells for them, their Denise Robinses (they called her Dennis), their Barbara Cartlands. They were always grateful: 'Thanks ever so much, duck!' I was once asked for Cartland's books by an earnest old girl—she was probably about fifty—who wanted them for her daughter who was about to be married. 'They learn you, y' know,' she assured me. I've often wondered how that marriage panned out.

The men who came in often asked for Westerns or mysteries. Quite a few of the local upper crust came in too, usually the wives, who would take out our more literary fiction, biographies, and travel books and order books they had seen reviewed in *The Times*. When the notorious *Forever Amber* finally reached Belper from Headquarters—it had been delayed because everyone at HQ had read it before it was sent into the hinterland—the list of requests was in the hundreds, and everyone, from the nattering old ladies to the nobs, would demand, 'How's the list for *Amber* getting on?' Because the list was so long, instead of being issued for a fortnight, we allowed only one week at a time. People with no neighbourhood library, who relied on a monthly issue of books sent to their local council rooms from Headquarters, had to wait even longer for it. Kathleen Winsor's famous novel could be called a bodice ripper, although it would appear very tame to a modern reader. Three million copies of the book were eventually sold.

⚜

After the war, when I was seventeen, my parents began to include me when Dad went to London for his business conferences. Gladys's wartime job had ended two years before, the sisters had agreed to forget their quarrel, and our aunt had come home to help take care of my brothers and sister so that my mother was free for a few days. Dad's firm met annually in various towns, and one year we stayed in great splendour at the Waldorf Hotel on the Strand. During the day, Mum and I were on our own to wander about London, its shops, and historic places. A couple of country bumpkins, neither of us had a good sense of direction, and we even had difficulty finding the Tower.

It was when we were on this excursion that we received an invitation from Buckingham Palace, not to take tea with the Queen, but a summons from Uncle Gib's sister, Aunt Madge, who was a Palace housekeeper. This was too good to miss, and with the halting of many a passer-by to ask for directions, Mum and I managed to find our way down the Mall to a side entrance of the Queen's residence, where a policeman, after checking with Aunt Madge, allowed us through the gates and into 'below stairs'.

Although Uncle Gib often spoke of his sister, we had not yet met Madge Dewar. Like him she was large and wide, and she sat in her own sitting room as if she were the queen herself. She made us very welcome in her good Scots tongue—which had its tart side. Before we had come to London, I had blown what seemed to me a great deal of money (ten pounds) on what was called a 'New Look' dress. The New Look came in about 1948, when material became a little more available. Skirts had become longer, to calf length; bodices and sleeves were very tight-fitting. My dress was tartan in different shades of brown and cream; I thought it made me look most elegant. So much so, that I had refused to hide it beneath a coat for our walk to the Palace, with the result that as the afternoon wore on, I had become chilled to the bone. Aunt Madge took one look at my blue lips and nodded. 'Aye,' she said confidingly to my mother, 'pride knows no cold.' How right she was.

To thaw me out, she served us hot tea, and afterwards she asked if we would like a tour of the palace. This was almost sixty years before the palace was opened to the public, so we were thrilled. Aunt Madge made enquiries of a passing footman as to where 'they' were, and upon receiving the reply that they were at dinner, she took us up a back staircase into the royal apartments. We saw everything: the sitting rooms, the bedrooms, and the staterooms. I have a memory of the sort of area one might see in a museum behind barriers: curved, rather uncomfortable Mme Recamier-style sofas; a lot of gilt on the furniture, many heavy portraits in oils on the walls. When, later, I described to Pete, now fourteen, how Aunt Madge had shown us both the King's and the Queen's bedrooms, he exclaimed, 'Gosh. Don't they sleep together?' We also passed near where the royals were taking dinner with a group of foreign diplomats, footmen in velvet knee breeches carrying salvers in and out of the room. This little royalist was thrilled to the marrow. (Odd how far to the left I lean in my later years—one is supposed to tip in the opposite direction, the older one becomes.)

These trips to London were, I suppose, pretty small beer, but I felt I had reached the apex of sophistication when I was taken to see *Oklahoma!* I loved the show's verve and was particularly intrigued when tea and biscuits were served to our seats during the interval, which made for a certain amount of discreet clattering during the second act. Some years later, after Princess Elizabeth was married to Prince Philip, I again travelled to the big city, this time on a bus named My Lady Coach from Crich, to see the Royal Wedding Presents (yes, with those capitals). Ah, the follies of one's—Conservative—youth.

By this time, around 1948, Europe was beginning to open up again. For some time I had been writing to a young French girl,

Ginette Brault, who lived in Loches, in the Department of Indre et Loire. Her high school and Margaret's had an exchange program in which the pupils wrote to each other, the French in English, the English in French, as so-called pen pals. There were more pupils attending Ginette's lyceé than there were at Margaret's Strutt's School in Belper, and Margaret had asked if I would write to one of the French girls who had no writing partner. This resulted in visits back and forth, and in 1947, Ginette and her friend Gill Coudert came over to visit us at Ballantrae House. Ginette soon became one of the family: helping in the kitchen, pulling Pete's leg, and calling Gib 'My 'usband'. He was seven and loved every minute of the attention. Ginette and her husband, Georges, continued to visit 'Mam and Dad Wallis' after I had moved to America; in 2008, they made a special trip to Derbyshire to visit my husband's grave at Crich.

The River Dove

I took the two French girls everywhere: by bus to Dove Dale, Chatsworth and Haddon Hall; to Crich for the view from the top of the Stand; to Stanton Moor and Dove Dale for picnics. I even took them to church, which was a big mistake. The trouble was, that as soon as Jean Barber's back was turned, I had stopped being a Primitive Methodist and now stayed home most Sundays. When I had invited my guests to accompany me to St Mary's C.of E. church at Crich, I had given no thought to what they believed, if anything. It turned out that Gill was a devout Catholic, and Ginette not much of anything. In any case, because I had been a Primitive Methodist, I was unsure where in the Church of England service I should stand up or kneel down, and since both Ginette and Gill were watching me for clues, I found that we were bobbing up and down like yo-yos, often out of sync with the rest of the congregation.

The next year, Margaret had just finished her Sixth Form year at Strutt's and was waiting to go to a teacher's training college in the autumn. I was working at the library and had garnered enough leave to make up a fortnight; it was time to make our first visit to France—after we had gathered together sufficient money for the trip. The fare, by train to Dover, a ferry to Calais, followed by a train to Paris and another south to Tours, would cost each of us ten pounds (the price of my New Look dress). At first, this seemed impossible, until my father presented me with a ten-pound note, after which Mr Gratrix, determined not to be outdone, did the same for Margaret.

Somehow or other, we two hobbledehoys managed to get ourselves over the Channel by ferry, by train to Paris, and across Paris to the Gare d'Austerlitz. Our French was of the schoolgirl variety, and in Paris we got into an altercation with a taxi driver, probably because we hadn't tipped him enough. However, somehow we made it to the station, bought tickets, and off we went south to Tours where we were met by Ginette, Gill, and Gill's brother, Colin.

It became obvious at once that, by our standards, Gill's family was quite well off—they owned a local bus company—while Ginette's widowed mother was just getting by. Mme Brault, though welcoming, was a tall, thin, and extremely nervous woman. She spoke no English, and since my French was better than Margaret's, I did most of the talking. M Brault, I gathered, had been a schoolteacher and had died sometime during the war. The Brault's house was in the Rue Jeanne d'Arc, part of a row of houses next door to a baker's shop from which, very early in the morning, wafted delicious smells. There were two bedrooms, with a double bed, a chest of drawers, and a statue of a small boy that sat on the bedside table. The toilet was primitive, with a metal contraption inside it that would tip when a lever was pulled, sliding its contents into a hole in a rush of water. Next to it was a tiny bathroom. There was no garden at the back, and the front door opened onto the street.

Mme Brault and Mme Coudert arranged that we should take our lunch and a lighter evening meal chez Coudert, our breakfast chez Brault. The Couderts' home was an eye-opener. They lived in what seemed to us an enormous house in a square at the centre of town. It had a balcony overlooking the square with a small yard in front and a garden to the rear, but what impressed us most about chez Coudert was the fact that they employed both a maid and a cook. The dining room was splendid, the food lavish; it seemed especially so when we compared our meagre post-war rations with the feast that appeared on the Couderts' table.

The first night we dined with them, I tasted my first, and last, snails, which Gill's brother persuaded us to eat by assuring us that they were kidneys. It was only after Margaret and I had each eaten two of them, whispering to one another that it was like chewing balls of rubber, that Colin asked the maid to show us the bucket into which she had thrown the shells.

Every time we ate at the Couderts', we English, young and quite unused to wine, became rather the worse for wear and, giggling wildly, staggered home to the Braults' house, which fortunately was not far away. 'Les petites anglaises sont toujours heureuses!' Mme Brault would exclaim innocently. One particularly drunken evening, Margaret and I fell on the bed in fits of laughter, and the statue at the bedside joined my earlier talking horse when it smiled at me beatifically.

And, of course, Gill and Ginette took us everywhere. Gill had her own car and drove us to every chateau within a fifty-mile radius: Amboise, Chinon, Azay-le-Rideau, Chenonceaux; to sulky races, the jockeys pulled along in light carriages behind their horses; and to swim in a lake in the nearby forest. We also met Jacques Coutourier, Gill's fiancé, a glum-faced man who was probably aware that he was Gill's second choice. It was to be a sad marriage; Gill had been engaged to another man who had died just after the war, and she had not recovered from the loss. She and Jacques remained married and had a daughter,

Kathy, but Gill had at least one lover that I know of, and possibly Jacques did also.

Margaret and I were to have other holidays together. We visited Polbae Cottage, the home of Aunt Rose and Uncle Gib Dewar, in Scotland, and also went further north, to Crieff, where we stayed with two more Dewar aunts, Maggie and Phemie (Euphemia). At the time, I was in love with James Graham, Marquis of Montrose, circa 1645, and the area had been one of his stamping grounds. (I had graduated from mysteries and was by then an avid reader of historical novels.) We also visited Portsmouth on the south coast, where old friends of the Gratrix family welcomed us. The man of the house was in the Royal Navy, and I was astonished to find that men who had been at sea were not above doing a little Hoovering or washing-up. We visited the port on Navy Day and went aboard a submarine; a most claustrophobic experience, even though the sub was in dock.

In the years after the war, of course, the other children in the family were growing up and beginning to twine it in. Pete left Bailey's early and went to work as a puddler in an iron foundry further down the valley. Puddlers work with molten metal; my parents' dreams of an office job for Pete would have to wait. Because he was a working man, he always came home ravenous, even after devouring the whole loaf's worth of sandwiches Mum packed for his lunch. At teatime, he was again ready for a huge fry-up. Pete worked in other capacities for the metal industry after this, finally becoming, like his father, a commercial traveller.

Peter Wallis (left) and fellow soldier

When Beryl left school, she took a job working as a drafts-woman for Glowworm, a company in Milford that made fires and other electrical appliances. From an extremely pretty small girl with fair curls and huge green eyes, my sister had grown into a very beautiful young woman.

Beryl (Wallis) Taylor

After school, Gib took a variety of jobs. His first was working at Smedley's foundry in Belper, after which he moved to Smalley's, the fruit and vegetable merchants, driving their lorries to Smithfield market in London and other places. Later, he was employed in greengrocer's shops, and towards the end of his life bought a shop of his own in a small town near Birmingham. Unfortunately, he went bankrupt after a chain store opened nearby, and he returned to Derbyshire where he kept afloat with his pension and by selling second-hand goods at car-boot sales. As a baby, Gib's hair had been almost white, his eyes large and green; like Uncle Bud, he was another family Swede.

CHAPTER 28

Courting at Last

BY 1947 I HAD reached my late teens. I still lived at home and enjoyed my work at the library, my courses in library science at the Tech, and the company of my friends. I was content. My mother, however, was again becoming agitated; her eldest daughter wasn't courting. She was so focused on this lack that I kept all my dates quiet, pretending to be going to the pictures with Betty from the library, or Josephine, a friend from my years at Bailey's, when in reality I was roaring off on the back of someone's motorbike à la Gladys, or going to the pictures with some youth I had met at a dance. None of these relationships was in the least important to me, and I was determined not to subject the hapless youths to scrutiny by Mum. What I actually wanted to do was finish my FLA (Fellow of the Library Association) degree and get another, better-paying job.

About this time, I was in charge of Belper's travelling library. The van was pretty much like the ones used nowadays—that is, as big as a mobile home, with shelves on three of its sides for books and a counter behind the driver's seat where I checked them out.

I was on the road five days a week and spent Saturday mornings at the library to restock the mobile's shelves and search out any requested books. We went round the west side of Derbyshire, almost to Ashbourne in the southwest and Alderwasley to the

Brenda in the Library Van

north, visiting farms and little villages I had never seen before. My readers were happy to see the van, many of them because they had no car, and buses to nearby towns ran at most once a week. On two of the routes, a reader often brought out a tray of coffee and biscuits for the driver and me, and most of them were anxious for a chat. Farmers' wives often gave us a few eggs, which were still scarce. (After the war a dreadful substance, dried egg, was introduced to fill the gaps in our rations.)

And then one Saturday, when I was helping behind the counter at Belper, a young man came in. I had not seen him in the library before, but I knew him at once; he was Joe Smith, the little green-eyed lad who had sat in front of me at Fritchley School. He looked very 'Cambridge', in flannel bags and a tweed jacket, with his college scarf flung casually round his neck and over one shoulder. He had no idea who I was, although he later claimed he was smitten at once.

A few days later, he came into the library again. I had cycled to work that day, and when I left and was riding past an old quarry outside the town, he was there with his bike, waiting in ambush. I put on a spurt, whipped down Matlock Road, paid a visit to Margaret, and waited there until my pursuer was long gone. (Today, he would probably be arrested as a stalker.)

Another evening, however, Joe caught up with me, and as we wheeled our bicycles up the Bottom Hag, he at last discovered that he knew me after all. It turned out that on that first evening in the library, he had assumed I must be an upper-class girl from Duffield and so had done his stakeout in the wrong direction.

As we walked, we made stilted conversation during which I asked if he were on holiday. 'We call it the vac, actually,' he told me, very 'Cambridge'. (This has become another family joke.) At the time I thought, sceptically, Mam-like, 'Oh, aye?'

Joe Smith at Cambridge University

Nevertheless, Joe and I met again, and then again, and before I knew where I was, we were 'courting.' We attended dances held at the Crich schoolroom where Joe's mother had worked as a teacher before her marriage. There, we shuffled around the school's uneven floorboards to the lugubrious strains of Beardmore's Band, with me trying to lead as I had been taught at grammar school, and closely watched by members of the village Women's Institute. These worthies doubled as refreshment ladies, serving tea, sandwiches, and cakes at long tables throughout the evening, Joe's Aunt Dora among them. Later that evening, my Aunt Flo cut in as we were dancing and waltzed off with my partner, quizzing him the while. Relationships in small villages are never private.

Dances then were for all ages, from ten-year-olds to those of sixty and seventy, and it was not unusual to see two elderly grannies, or two teenage girls dancing together. The four-piece band played waltzes interspersed with a few quicksteps, to which the show-offs jitterbugged in the corners. These were largely sedate occasions, although after ten o'clock, when the pubs closed, we were invariably invaded by inebriated youths and even older men reeking of beer, who trod heavily on our toes with their farm boots. The last waltz was always the lugubrious 'With someone like you/A pal good and true/I plan to leave it all behind...'

During our courtship, Joe and I hiked all over Derbyshire: the Dales, the moors, and the canal towpaths. We walked from Crich over the moors to Matlock, where we had tea at the Cinema Cafe at the bottom of Steep Turnpike, and to the Bear Inn near Alderwasley, where we listened on the wireless to the boat race between Oxford and Cambridge, cheering as the Oxford boat sank. We went to Derby County football games, where Joe was afraid I'd be shocked when a man behind us yelled 'Get t'bloody ball in't bloody goal, you daft bugger!' I rather enjoyed the match. I don't think we ever went to the pictures.

Eventually I decided that I had to take this one home. Mum was busy digging in the garden when we arrived, and with what was to me embarrassing speed, she cleaned her fork and hurried inside to make us tea and sandwiches. She was determined not to let this one get away. I had made no preliminary arrangements with her for the visit, although I had made sure that Peter would be out, because I was not ready for the teasing that was bound to ensue if he were home. However, it proved even more embarrassing to see how pleased, and even eager, my mother was that her daughter had brought a young man home to tea, at last! Being invited to a boyfriend or girlfriend's home for tea was known locally as 'getting your feet under t'table'. Mum made us ham sandwiches with mustard, which we both disliked, but we ate them, nonetheless. Beryl and Gib were not at home, and Dad was still at work, so we got away almost scot-free on that occasion.

I was afterwards invited to Joe's parents' home at Barn Close Farm so that they could vet me. Mrs Smith had already told my mother that she and her husband were 'that pleased it's your Brenda. We'd been afraid he'd bring one of those foreigners home from Cambridge'. I'm not sure what she meant by foreigners, although I suspect she meant someone from another county and with a posh accent, rather than someone from abroad. I hadn't met any of the Smiths at that time, apart from Joe's younger brother, Tom, having spent an evening with him and another friend when we drove about the village in 'The Grey Ghost', as the Smiths called their car, putting up posters advertising a Conservative Party rally.

This didn't save me from Tom's teasing, but Mrs Smith kept him fairly well under control, until I had to ask to visit the lavatory. This was outside across the back yard, and because there was no electricity in the house, Joe had to light a lantern to show me the way. 'Ayup! Is 'e gooin' wi' 'er?' asked Tom. Despite this episode, the visit wasn't too difficult for me because, in addition to Joe, Mr and Mrs Smith, and Tom, seated around the tea table were Joe's youngest siblings, Frank and Hilary. Joe's sister, nine, with stiff, fair pigtails, and Frank, a dark, gangly lad of fourteen, were suffused in giggles and purple with embarrassment. This made me feel much more in charge of the situation, and because my future in-laws made me welcome, the occasion passed off well.

Aunt Dora and Uncle Bill Leese

I also went to be scrutinized by Joe's Aunt Dora and Uncle Bill at Ashbourne House in Crich; Aunt Dora was Mr Smith's sister. Ashbourne House had been the Smith family home for some time and was next door to the woodworking and builder's shop, where several members of the family and about thirty employees from the village made coffins and furniture. Joe's Uncle Norman was in charge of the business.

Aunt Dora and Uncle Bill were very welcoming, but their daughter Jenny was also present, and judging by her look of glum fury, she was either very shy or else disapproved of me mightily. (On remembering myself at her age, I wonder now if she'd had a child's crush on her cousin.) In any case, she sat on a sort of tuffet and scowled all evening, although later we became friends.

I also visited Joe in Cambridge several times, taking the London train from Derby to Huntingdon, where I changed to a little train that chugged slowly through the mild countryside, stopping at every station to deliver letters, parcels, chickens, or a few passengers. Joe was busy finishing his PhD and hadn't a lot of time for 'vacs' in Derbyshire. The room I stayed in was the usual rather dismal student digs, but Cambridge showed me a world where it was possible for a young woman to be emancipated and free, which made my sheltered existence seem tame. During my visits, Joe and I did all the Cambridge things, including punting along the Backs as far as Grantchester to take tea in the nearby orchard where Rupert Brooke, Virginia Woolf, and others of the Bloomsbury group used to meet. I loved Cambridge; it was a whole new world to me with its little teashops, its glorious historic buildings and their gardens, its streets crammed with students in their short gowns (compulsory wear at the time), and its myriad bicycles.

During Joe's next visit home, his PhD degree completed, he informed me that he had received an offer of a three-year 'post doc' position at the Geophysical Lab, part of the Carnegie Institution in Washington, D.C., and was I willing to marry him and take off over the Atlantic for a while? Yes, reader, I married him, but first, because we lived in antediluvian times, Joe was faced with the task of asking my father's permission. I don't know which of them looked forward to the encounter the least, but one evening, just after Dad had come home from his nightly visit to The King's Arms and we guessed he would be in a jovial mood, Joe bearded him. If Dad was dismayed by how little Joe had in the bank, he didn't say so. I had virtually nothing saved and was still earning a pittance at the library; even so, Dad said yes. The lad, after all, had potential.

Now I was stuck with buying things for my 'bottom drawer', a task I had determinedly avoided. At the time, girls were supposed to begin accumulating sheets, pillowcases, and household implements of every sort from the age of thirteen on, to be ready for that long-awaited day when they were brides. But the war had intervened, and goods of any sort became scarce. I hadn't been enthusiastic about filling my bottom drawer in any case because I was going to be Head Librarian, and by the time my mother finally thought she'd manoeuvred me into doing my duty, household items were scarcer than ever. This meant that by our wedding day, I had accumulated only a couple of sheets, two dubious-looking blankets, and an eggbeater. The blankets (which I still have) were of a dull gold colour, and bore on their hems a couple of black half circles, the wartime Utility Mark.

St Mary's Church, Crich

On August 31, 1951, Joe and I made our separate ways to St Mary's Parish Church in Crich. It was a dark, rainy morning, but guests and family had already gathered, and the pews were almost full when I arrived. Joe was waiting near the altar steps beside his brother Tom, who was to be his Best Man; I, with my attendants, Joe's sister Hilary and my sister Beryl, waited shivering in the draughty porch. The vicar failed to appear. After much telephoning, my mother-in-law discovered that the Reverend H E Jones (High Explosive was his nickname—he was anything but) had left for parts unknown and had asked the vicar from the nearby village of Holloway to preside in his place. The man had forgotten and had just begun to eat lunch when we phoned him, which meant we had to wait another three-quarters of an hour for him to show up.

After that, everything had to go splendidly, and it did. We took our vows, which included my reluctant promise to obey, and to which I added the internal rider: 'it depends'.

My mother-in-law had chosen the necessary hymns for us after vainly waiting for me to do so. I'd had trouble making up my mind about this since the hymns I had learned with the Primitive Methodists struck me as foreign to the Church of England. However, since Joe came from a farming family, Mother Smith had chosen 'We Plough the Fields, and Scatter', and because Joe and I were shortly to be taking our lives into our hands by venturing over the Atlantic on board the *Queen Mary*, 'For Those in Peril on the Sea'. In either case, I don't think she intended to be humourous. (In regard to the photo, taken outside the Hurt Arms, stakes driven through both the bride's and the groom's heads were not part of the ceremony.)

The reception went off in rollicking fashion with the Best Man making the expected speech, and the uncles, Joe's and mine, knocking back a considerable amount of beer. Afterwards, I noticed my father and father-in-law in an argument. 'My lot drank more than your lot, Jack,' my father-in-law was insisting as he thrust a ten-pound note at my father, who refused to take it. It fell to the floor and lay there until, as though reluctantly, my father stooped, picked up the note, and stuffed it into his pocket. Dad was always a prudent man.

So it was, that after a rainy two-week honeymoon in Cornwall, followed by excursions to Derby to look for suitcases and a steamer trunk into which to pack our few belongings, we bid a tearful goodbye to our numerous family members and set off on our perilous journey to spend three years in America.

At least, that was the plan.

The Queen Mary

Made in the USA
Middletown, DE
02 November 2022